Outlining Goes Electronic

ATTW Contemporary Studies in Technical Communication

M. Jimmie Killingsworth, Series Editor

Published in cooperation with the Association of Teachers of Technical Writing

Outlining Goes Electronic

by
Jonathan Price
The Communication Circle

Volume 9 in ATTW Contemporary Studies in Technical Communication

Ablex Publishing Corporation
Stamford, Connecticut

Printed in the United States of America

The author gratefully acknowledges that portions of this material appeared, in earlier drafts, in *Computers and Composition* and the *IEEE Transactions on Professional Communication.* The editors Stuart Selber, Anne Hill Duin, and Scott Sanders—offered much kind and thoughtful advice.

Library of Congress Cataloging-in-Publication Data

Price, Jonathan, 1941-
    Outlining goes Electronic / by Jonathan Price.
    p.   cm. — (ATTW contemporary studies in technical
        communications; v. 9)
        Includes bibliographical references and index.
    ISBN 1-56750-378-0 (cloth). — ISBN 1-56750-379-9 (pbk.)
    1.   English language—Technical English—Computer programs.
2. Technical writing—computer programs.   3. Outlines—Computer
programs.   I. Title.   II. Series

PE1475.P75   1999
808'.066—dc21

99-51776
CIP

Ablex Publishing Corporation
100 Prospect Street
P.O. Box 811
Stamford, CT 06904-0811

to Lisa, with love

Contents

Part II: A Look Back

Part III: Summing Up

Acknowledgments

I want to thank Scott Sanders and Jimmie Killingsworth for their wise guidance as I shaped and reshaped this book; they have helped me rethink and reorganize the material so that it is far clearer than before. David Farkas also contributed immensely with his detailed questions and suggestions. The comments of Anne Hill Duin and Stuart Selber helped me clarify and simplify the discussion of outlining in the classroom. Conversations with Chuck Campbell, Lynn Deming, and Emily Nye have also helped me think through my position on outlining as a form of collaboration.

I owe much of my early thinking on outlining and collaboration to extended conversations with Henry Korman, my co-author in *How to Communicate Technical Information* (1993), and my partners: Elaine Pendergast, Lisa Price, Mick Renner, Adam Rochmes, and Linda Urban. I have also learned enormously from collaborating on books and articles with Steve Anderson, Weifeng Bao, Suzanne Brown, Chuck Campbell, Marty Downey, David Gillette, Nancy Hindle, John Lahr, Subhasish Mazumdar, Tom Outler, Randy Scasny, Carlene Schnabel, and Zhengang Yao. My ideas of collaboration also owe an enormous amount to Jack Jorgens, the Shakespearean scholar, Joel Katz, the photographer and designer, my fellow artists in the Westbroadway Gallery, a cooperative gallery in New York City, the many participants in the Association of Artist-Run Galleries, and my collaborators on the Wall project at Pleiades Gallery—Joellen Bard, Marilyn Belford, Ken Glickfeld, Jerry Herman, and E. S. Pearlman.

And I am deeply indebted to the many writers—beginners and professionals—who have participated in my classes and workshops; their questions and observations have continually shaped my thinking about the extraordinary impact that media have on our ideas of outlining and the collaborative conversation. Finally, I want to thank my friends, who have so kindly supported me in this long campaign to clarify our thinking about structure.

Preface

This little book examines a writing activity that has recently fallen into disrepute. Outlining has a bad reputation among students, even though many teachers and textbooks still recommend the process. In part, the medium is to blame: Paper and ink make revision difficult, because one must recopy so much information, but particularly if one uses an electronic outliner, the activity can be very helpful in developing a thoughtful and effective document, particularly one that spans many pages and deals with a complicated subject.

Technical writers who must create structures for vast systems of information often use visual displays of hierarchical information to create structures that users can easily understand and navigate. When these writers discover electronic outlining, many adopt it as a tool, because it provides many of the benefits our teachers claimed for outlining, without the tedious and messy activities we faced when trying to revise a paper outline.

In addition, electronic outlining turns out to be an efficient way to focus a meeting on developing an agreed-upon structure for a document. In effect, making the outline fluid, the software offers a way to record new contributions, modifications, reorganization, as a group moves toward greater understanding of its material, its goals, and each other. What electronic outlining demonstrates so visibly, then, is that in writing we are always involved in a larger conversation.

PART I: THE SITUATION TODAY

I begin this book considering the current state of outlining—a process that has provoked controversy in disciplines as widely dispersed as technical writing and composition. Instead of starting with the history, as one might expect, I start with the present, and work backwards. Part I considers the nature of a new tool, the electronic outliner, software that enables restructuring a document on the computer, and, surprisingly, encourages collaborative work on large, complex documents, as well.

Chapter 1: A Little Context

In the first chapter, I sketch the origin of electronic outlining, and suggest that the change from paper and pen to electronics has profound implications for our understanding of the document we call an outline, and the activities that take place during the process of outlining. I summarize the rather skimpy theory of outlining as it emerged from the process movement, who seem to have reacted quite strongly to the school model of "the outline." More recently, other researchers have begun to suggest that outlining can be seen as an important activity within the recursive and overlapping processes of researching, planning, and drafting. I argue that the switch to electronic outlining integrates outlining much more thoroughly into the whole writing process, from start to finish. And, just as hypertext tools have enabled greater collaborative work than was possible with ink and paper, I suggest that electronic outlining may provide another tool for the social construction of knowledge. Reflecting on my own experience creating documentation for major computer companies, I argue that electronic outlining, in fact, can form an even more useful collaborative tool for creating the kind of vast and complex information systems that technical writers are today called on to prepare.

Chapter 2: How Electronic Outlining Helps Writers Turn Structuring into a Continuous Process

What exactly is involved in electronic outlining? Because most people are familiar with word processing, but only a fraction of those have used the electronic outlining modules within their word processing applications, I describe exactly what the electronic outlining software does. It makes possible extensive and wide-ranging work on developing the structure of a document—particularly valuable when the writer is preparing a large document, such as a CD-ROM, a Help system, or a Web site, with information that changes from day to day, in a team with several other writers and folks from other disciplines. With dozens of functions that allow the most common structuring activities of ordinary thought, outlining software allows a writer to consider alternate structures quickly, make changes without being distracted by a need to reformat or recopy, and switch to note-taking or drafting when inspired, without leaving the electronic document. Outlining, then, becomes a view of the material, a structural perspective, always available, encouraging continuous consideration of organization. The result, particularly when done in a team, is a structure that has been so thoroughly edited that it seems clear, even self-evident, to the person who must use the document.

Chapter 3: Extending the Collaborative Conversation

Electronic outlining software is also an excellent collaborative tool for people who are meeting face to face, whether in a classroom or in an office. In this chapter, I distinguish several kinds of group work, focusing on full, person-to-person collaboration. I summarize the ways in which electronic outlining software encourages social routines for this kind of work together. Two examples flesh out this description: In one, a team develops the table of contents for a technical manual, and in the other, I lead a class in working together to create an outline together. The instantaneous display of each contribution, the ease with which the group can rework the organization, and the way in which the changeable display serves to focus the group conversation, all help the participants work together, then reflect on the way in which they have created a document that no one person owns, but that reflects their best thoughts, as a group. In this way, the process gives students an example of social construction of knowledge, and an opportunity to think about it, based on their own experience.

PART II: A LOOK BACK

Having described how electronic outlining software works, and how it can contribute to collaborative construction of knowledge, I look back at the school model of "the outline." The new, electronic process serves as a bright background against which I silhouette the ideas and practices many of us took for granted when we lumbered through outlining in school. In these two chapters, I highlight the degree to which the older model derived, unconsciously for the most part, from the media it assumed—ink and paper.

Chapter 4: The Paper Model

Few people in the last century have reasoned very much about outlines, but the tradition of assigning outlines in school indicates how important many teachers considered outlines, as a device for improving the structure of their student's documents. Because we have no formal theory of outlines, I turn to more than 50 years of textbooks for the picture of the outline being presented by their authors— a practitioners' model. The medium heavily influences their image of the outline. So I begin with a quick media history of the outline, showing how it may have evolved from ancient times, propelled by the shift from papyrus rolls to vellum sheets bound into books, and then, in the renaissance, by the availability of paper, printing presses, and the arguments of schoolmen like Erasmus and Ramus. In the 17th and 18th centuries, Puritan ministers seem to have adopted Ramus' method of outlining, and early scientists adopted the technique, as well. By the 19th century, Darwin and other scientists took taxonomic hierarchies—and verbal outlines—as a standard way of organizing vast bodies of information. Similarly, rhetoricians gradually embedded outlining in their courses. For most of the 20th century, outlines have been an accepted assignment in schools and colleges.

Just as notes acquired their own paper format—notecards—outlines became standardized on paper sheets, to judge from the textbooks of the last half century. As a result of the medium, and the constraints it imposed, textbook authors describe the outline as a discreet document, different from notes, and different from a draft. (In the light of our computer screen, we now can see that the same electronic document can handle all three aspects of writing—displaying an outline view, a text view, and a set of notes that can then be hidden, when not needed.) One consequence of the idea that an outline is a discreet document is the misconception that structuring forms a distinct stage. First one outlines, then one writes. This neat paradigm, which was popularized by Warriner (1950), but subscribed to by textbook authors until well into the 1990s, ignores the reality that most writers do a little planning, then a little research, then a little drafting, and so back through the loop in a very untidy process, in which the evolving outline is just part of the way the writer thinks.

Few textbook authors imagine that the outline can grow continuously throughout the project, probably because such real work on structure involves multiple passes through the material—something that becomes quite tedious when recopying a pencilled outline on paper. This unacknowledged difficulty may be why most authors do not consider research as part of outlining, and limit the "writing" in an outline to achieving parallel form. For these authors, if new ideas come up after the outline is "finished," the ideas must be incorporated into the draft—one simply cannot go back and update the outline. And if the draft has completely gotten out of hand, one may make up a brand new outline, to analyze its structure—but, being paper, this new outline is an entirely separate document from the original outline, and the draft.

Even when confronted with the arrival of the typewriter on college campuses, and then by word processing, many textbook authors remain quite innocent of the influence the media may have had on their ideas. Twenty-five years after the arrival of word processing, a dozen years after outlining software appeared, the textbook authors continue to write as if an outline is an outline, no matter what medium it is created in. The failure to deal thoughtfully with the fact that most students use word processing indicates the degree to which the textbook authors are still attached to the earlier, paper model.

Chapter 5: Why Outline?

Given how hard it is to revise a paper outline, I am not surprised that most students came to dislike outlining, but most textbook authors still felt outlines could be useful, and their arguments on behalf of the activity reveal several real benefits that students could have had, if they had bothered to spend much time doing the outlines that were assigned.

The first benefit is intellectual: Doing an outline improves the logic of one's document. I hear overtones of discipline envy here—wishing that writing had some of the glamour of engineering, science, or mathematics, but the authors are also expressing, in their emphasis on the idea of logic, that structuring our material is a form of thinking.

The second group of benefits is practical: Outlining saves time and money. True enough, if done.

The third group of benefits is described through metaphor, suggesting the less tangible, but still strongly felt reasons for outlining. Authors talk, at last, of making structure visible, the way an architect does with a plan; they stress that this work involves envisioning, seeing in the mind's eye, and creating. On the analogy of a skeleton, other authors stress the organic whole one can achieve through this work on structure, and a few even talk romantically of the way the whole grows from seed to living form.

Such were the dreams of the textbook authors, the deep currents driving them to recommend outlining, even when the media they inherited—paper and ink—prevented many students from getting these benefits. I argue that electronic outlining makes many of these payoffs possible.

PART III: SUMMING UP

Having looked at electronic outlining, and looked back at the school model, I pull together a theory of outlining that takes the media into account. I use the contrast between the paper and the electronic model as the basis for a synthesis that, I hope, sheds light on the important function of structuring, when we write.

Chapter 6: Toward a New Model of Outlining

Media make a huge difference to our conception of the process and product of creating a verbal structure. I summarize the differences between the paper and electronic models, then draw out the implications. I argue that there is no such thing as outlining, free of a particular medium. The medium is determinative, constraining and allowing the activities one can carry out, and the end results—hence, one's ideas and images of what has gone on.

In outlining, then, we turn to some external medium to fix our current thoughts about structure so we can analyze and improve them. In this sense, the outline—in whatever medium—acts as a surrogate for our own previous best thought, encouraging a conversation with ourselves, or with our partners if we are in a collaborative team. As we do more research, we hear other voices; as we debate with other people, we change our own ideas—and the evolving outline may reflect that turn of the conversation as well. Any moment's outline provides a focus for the talk, an aid to memory, and a record of the conversation "up to now," but it also makes visible that the document we see growing in front of us is truly a collaborative effort, a pulling together of many voices, a symbol of our effort to reach agreement and understanding. We may never "reach" a structure that perfectly represents the information we are puzzling over, but the outline leads us on, if the media are sociable enough, and the tools are convivial, encouraging further consideration. In the end, we are left with the conversation, and its luminous artifact.

I

The Situation Today

1

A Little Context

I n this book, I develop a theoretical model of outlining as an activity. I argue that a relatively new electronic tool—software that accelerates and transforms the process of outlining—can give us a new perspective from which to engage previous classroom models of writing, recent writing theory, and current practice in the technical writing field.

Outlining software may have gotten its start as a programming tool. In 1958 John McCarthy, a computer scientist, and Marvin Minsky, a mathematics professor, started the M.I.T. Artificial Intelligence Project, and working with a number of graduate students, began creating a programming language called LISP, which has several unusual features. Instead of doing calculations with numbers, LISP can manipulate symbolic expressions, such as those of IF-THEN conditions and Boolean logic. Better yet, LISP can accommodate a string of reasoning, in which the symbolic expressions are represented as a list. Within that list there can be multiple levels, so the content of one statement can easily be expanded by adding subtopics. Lists can be chained together with other lists; items can be inserted or deleted. With the addition of an interpreter on a time-sharing system, the language gained the ability to handle these manipulations without first recompiling a program, and then running it—making it possible to edit a list on the fly. (McCarthy, 1981). Later developers came up with an editor that would display the indented hierarchical lists as a programmer created them, to make the evolving structure clear, as it grew.

In the mid 1970s, Dave Winer, a student at the University of Wisconsin, saw a hierarchic program editor for the LISP language, and, inspired, created a similar tool for Pascal programmers. Winer (1988) recalls:

> This embryonic outliner could dive and surface, displaying one level of the hierarchy at a time. Programmers could edit the structure of their programs directly....This very early piece of software met the two criteria that make something an outliner: you can control the level of detail in the display of information, and you can reorganize according to the structure of the information. (n.p.)

Winer (1988) went on to develop outlining software that a consumer could use (VisiText™, funded by and then canceled by Personal Software, the makers of the original spreadsheet, VisiCalc™), a bulletin board system that used outlining to keep track of messages and threads, and, in 1983, a consumer product called ThinkTank™ for the Apple II™ computer, ported to the IBM PC and the Macintosh computers in 1984. Adding organization charts, bullets, slide shows, a calendar maker, a phone dialer, and graphic pizzazz, Winer and his brother Peter released a new version called MORE™ for the Macintosh in June 1986. "I look back on MORE as the perfect product," Winer (1988) says. "It took outline processing, which was still a very spacy sort of category in 1986, and transformed it into a business application" (n.p.)

Indeed, ThinkTank™ and MORE™ were then imitated and popularized by more than a dozen of the most popular and successful word processing programs, presentation packages, idea processors, and complex document processors. Going beyond a view of the document as running text or formatted pages, outlining software offers a structural perspective on the evolving document. As a "view," then, outlining software has become a component within the most widely used office programs in the world. Bolter (1991) comments, "It is no accident that the computer can serve as an outline processor. The machine is designed to create and track such formal structures" (p. 19), including hierarchies of programming structures such as lists, stacks, and branching trees, which are themselves outlines.

Heim (1993) raises the question, "What happens when computers supersede the printing press, when the outline is computerized?" (p. 46). His answer, in part, is that we evolve from a modern to a post-modern sensibility. Where the paper outline expresses an urge arising in the Renaissance, to "organize things visually in logical schemes" (p. 46), the electronic outliner shifts the focus from a fixed product to an ongoing process. "The spatial anatomy of an ideational sequence now turns fluid, dynamic, unconstrained, and users sense the difference immediately.

People familiar with grammar-school outlines lose their bias against outlining, their reluctance giving way to a feeling that computer outliners support their personal thought, fitting it like a second skin" (p. 47).

In this chapter, I provide a preliminary look at the new model of outlining, made possible by this genre of software. Then I summarize how writing theorists have dealt with outlining over the last quarter century. Finally, I describe how my own experience using electronic outlining to do technical writing has led me to consider this software a convivial tool for truly collaborative work.

THE MAIN IDEA: HOW GOING ELECTRONIC DEEPENS OUR UNDERSTANDING OF OUTLINING

Electronic outlining software helps writers incorporate structural analysis, design, and construction into the very process of writing. Automating a constellation of activities that were difficult to do on paper, the software shifts attention from product to process, makes that process easier to carry out, and allows writers to articulate their understanding of the many activities involved, while also facilitating a form of collaboration that would not have been possible on paper.

Outlining on the computer rather than on paper, one can create a much more visible hierarchy, not cramped by handwriting, tiny labels, and irregular indentation, and one can investigate it immediately by changing an item's level, phrasing, or position in sequence without recopying the rest of the outline, scribbling over, or drawing arrows. One sees the effect of any organizational change instantly. The sheer convenience encourages a more thorough exploration of the evolving structure as one discovers new ideas, revises parts of the organization, tries out some writing, and goes back to the subject-matter expert, documents, or Internet to do more research. Done by an individual in this way, electronic outlining becomes central to the writing process, instead of an annoying document required by some high school teacher. Electronic outlining becomes a way of viewing the material, getting a structural perspective, and thereby developing a more coherent interpretation.

When used in the workplace or classroom to focus and record an ongoing conversation, outlining software also encourages group collaboration in brainstorming, researching, organizing, and writing. The electronic nature of the medium lets a group record, change, debate, and review more ideas than they could handle on a blackboard or flipchart.

More important, electronic outlining can act as a sort of grown-up Lego™ set, representing and encouraging the thinking process by allowing participants to manipulate the ideas visually, re-ordering, re-sequencing, adding or subtracting, working up from the bottom, or drilling down from the top.

Outlining software, then, acts to externalize the process of structural revision, providing a temporary outline that represents "what we thought a minute ago," allowing participants to stand apart and carry on a conversation with their earlier positions. In this way, the software brings the internal conversation into the open. Used in a class, the software helps students "see" that they are, together, constructing a collective understanding, using the emerging outline as a placeholder for previous thoughts, another participant in the social construction of knowledge.

SITUATING THE OUTLINE IN THEORY

Electronic outlining makes the old critique of outlines by the process movement obsolete. In the 1970s and 1980s, scholarship on the pedagogy of arrangement tended to focus on the development of structure, rather than on outlining as a set of useful activities. Scholars argued that a concern for structure could take us beyond the patterns-of-development approach and contribute to the process (Coe, 1987; Enos, 1985; Hartwell, 1979; Knoblauch & Brannon, 1984; Olsen, 1989; Podis, 1980, Podis & Podis, 1990). Wary of offering an "outline" as a static arrangement promising students control over material, Podis and Podis (1990) even stressed their own anxiety, indecision, hemming and hawing, their own experience of being out of control, as they arranged their essay on arrangement.

In investigating the way writers plan their work, Hayes and Flower (1980) and Kaufer, Fleming, Werner, and Sinsheimer-Weeks (1986) suggested that after mentally mulling over the subject, a writer might write down a plan in an outline form. However, Flower and Hayes (1980, 1981a, 1981b) criticized the outline as a product-based plan, the kind of plan that occurs "when the composing process is governed by a concern for the form of the finished product" (1981b, p. 49), and suggested that the difficulty of producing a formal outline could slow the writer down. In 1984 they drew a distinction between fragmentary, vague, and incomplete plans for writing, which they saw as useful, and "more formal, logical, and limited 'plans,' associated with outlines and notes" (1984, p. 124). Stotsky (1990) pointed out that in much research on planning, the ideas of goals, plans, and strategies were conflated or left astonishingly vague. She concluded: "It is not clear what kind of plans the process of planning results in or how plans and goals may be distinguished from one another, if indeed they are distinct entities" (p. 42). She noted how practitioners applied theory and found similar confusion. Researchers on the composing process had also found that writers contemplating a short piece rarely outline (Bereiter & Scardamalia, 1987; Emig, 1971; Hillocks, 1986; Mischel, 1974; Perl, 1979; Pianko, 1979; Stallard, 1974), although writers facing a longer or more complex document often do (Emig, 1971; Kellogg, 1988, 1994; Kulthau, 1988; McCarthy, 1985; Nelson, 1992; Sommers & McQuade, 1984; Stein, 1990; Taylor & Beach, 1984). Elbow (1981) cautioned against trying to outline when one has no ideas on the subject, recommending free writing as a better way of discovering and inventing ideas. And several studies, taking off from the traditional model (outline first, then write) suggested that prewriting strategies may freeze a writer's thoughts (particularly if the writer doesn't have many, to begin with), preventing new ideas from arising during drafting (Galbraith, 1992; Hayes-Roth & Hayes-Roth, 1979; Horton, 1982). However, as Stotsky (1990) stated, "The practice of formal outlining recommended in traditional texts may be inhibiting" (p. 46).

Indeed, as we will see in Chapter 4, the traditional textbook model presented an outline as a single document, not as a process—a document decorated with typographical codes borrowed from mathematics and Latin, arranged in nested sequences that few students comprehend; a document, moreover, that acts as a rigid blueprint the student must follow when drafting, with any variations (or new ideas) being punished by the teacher as a violation of contract. In other words, the real purpose of outlining—to develop a meaningful structure for the document—became lost amid the use of paper (which made changing anything difficult) and pen (which afforded few ways of indicating hierarchy other than indentation and the extremely arbitrary typographical codes indicating levels and sequences), as well as a pedagogy favoring forms over process, and stressing individual work (one student, one outline) over group work. Daiute (1985) pinpointed the paper medium as a major obstacle to the formal outlining recommended universally by teachers and textbooks from the 1930s through the 1960s.

Influenced by cognitive psychologists' distinction between thinking and writing (Newell & Simon, 1972; Schank & Abelson, 1977), writing researchers have continued to consider an outline as a written-down thought rather than viewing the process of outlining as a way of thinking. Stotsky (1990) points out, "The interaction between thought and written language during the planning process may be the critical activity that determines the coherence of the first draft" (p. 49). She suggests a more intimate relationship between composing and drafting than cognitivists acknowledged, and, following Vygotsky, stresses that as writers think verbally, they move back and forth "between thought and visible (or audible) language" (Stotsky, 1990, p. 54).

In my experience, outlining electronically allows individuals and groups to think aloud, record their thoughts onscreen, analyze those thoughts as if they came from an "other," and collectively come to a new understanding. Outlining software also blurs old distinctions between planning, researching, and drafting. Although not directly dealing with outlines, most studies in the last 15 years have shown that the various processes involved in writing occur again and again, recursively overlapping, and frequently intersecting with each other (Beaugrande, 1984; Hult & Harris, 1987; Kellogg, 1994; Kennedy, 1985; Kostelnick, 1989a; McCutchen, 1986; Moberg, 1986; Schwartz, 1985). What's odd is that outlining gets mentioned so rarely in this discussion. Kellogg (1994) notes that "Research on outlining is limited" (p. 124). Reviewing observational and field research on prewriting, he says, "The only strong, positive effect is the correlation between outlining and productivity. The studies that yielded null or negative results all suffer from low statistical power, using in most cases only a handful of participants" (p. 125). To correct this gap in the research, Kellogg undertook a number of surveys and experiments. In interviewing science and engineering faculty he found that written outlining had a significant correlation with productivity (Kellogg, 1986, 1994). In fact, in another study, Kellogg (1988) showed that writers who had prepared an outline mentally or in writing were able to reduce attentional overload, when drafting, so they could concentrate substantially more on translating their ideas from the plan to written form, as Murray (1985) had suggested. Kellogg concluded that for long documents an external outline (written, not mental) would be critical, as Stotsky (1990) also argued.

Looking back over the same decades of research as Kellogg does, Walvoord and colleagues (1995) state, "In this body of research, outlining is either absent, conflated with other categories, classified in such a way as to obscure its unique features, specifically omitted from powerful writing processes, or negatively associated with linear or unproductive composing practices" (p. 393). They point out that Flower and Hayes (1977) attacked outlines as mere products, ignored their position as bridges between planning and writing, dismissed outlines as encouraging writers to "paint by numbers—to simply fill in the blanks" (p. 457), and condemned them as crutches and a straitjackets. Hillocks (1986) also dismissed such textbook mantras as "formulate a thesis, develop an outline, and write" (p. 27). However, Walvoord and colleagues (1995) state, "But now that the research so richly suggests the fluidity, complexity, and interconnectedness of writing processes and forms, it is time to unhitch the outline from its narrow textbook definition to explore how students actually use it, and to reconsider it in that context" (p. 394).

In their study of college students' development of complex papers in several disciplines, Walvoord et al. (1995) found that outlining appeared to be "a powerful strategy that cut across, participated in, and transcended individual processes such as planning or organizing [and served] multiple functions across a broad span of the writing process" (p. 418). Certainly, in my own experience, electronic outlining, as a process, evolves cyclically, almost randomly, affecting and strengthening all three activities—researching, organizing, and writing.

Just as the move to word processing encouraged and made more visible the social nature of writing (Costanzo, 1994; Duin & Hansen, 1994; Eldred, 1989; Hawisher, 1994; Humphrey, 1987; Rodrigues & Rodrigues, 1986), electronic outlining encourages a social perspective. Duin and Hansen (1994) define the social perspective this way:

> Social interaction can be seen as the mechanism for the process of social construction, the means by which individuals cooperate to construct and interpret reality, and a means by which individuals become literate....The basic idea of social construction is that groups of people, bound by shared experiences or interests, build meaning through an ongoing process of communication, interpretation, and negotiation. Facts, beliefs, truth itself result from a social process of conversation and consensus building. (pp. 90-91)

Because of rhetorical concerns with audience, much of the thinking in this field focuses on the conversation between the writer and the reader, as suggested by Bakhtin (1981, 1986), Bakhtin and Volosinov (1986), and Volosinov (1973). But with the increase of group writing, more scholars recognize that writing itself can be done collaboratively, as an extended conversation (Duin & Hansen, 1994; Ede & Lunsford, 1990). Unfortunately, few researchers have explored electronic outlining within this context.

Similarly, the electronic tools enabling groups to create hypertexts together foster the social construction of knowledge and text (Adelson & Jordan, 1992; Irish & Trigg, 1989), but, as Johnson-Eilola (1994) points out, most hypertext theorists have either disregarded the interplay of technology and social practice, or focused too exclusively on the technology (see also Hawisher, 1989, Kaplan, 1991). Johnson-Eilola (1994) remarks, "The social aspects of the construction of knowledge are not always visible to the participants" (p. 214). I argue that electronic outlining, used in the workplace and classroom, encourages social interaction as a group works out "what it knows," and makes that process visible.

In the context of the extensive scholarship on writing, then, outlining as an activity remains weakly theorized, and despite increased interest in word processing and hypertext, outlining on the computer has not been seriously explored for its full capabilities. Farkas (1995) called for more study of electronic outlining because he saw it as a valuable tool. In this book I provide some indication of the way electronic outlining works in industry and in the classroom as a device for thinking, as a facilitator of collaboration, and as an eye-opening representation of the social construction that goes on during collaborative writing. In the process, I must occasionally relate my own experiences, because they may serve as raw material for others to consider theoretically or pedagogically, and because, as Bleich (1995) says, "A pedagogy of individual and collective disclosure can help to revoke the polarization of the subjective and the collective as categories of experience. Such teaching can maintain the necessity of understanding the collective within the subjective, and the subjective within the collective" (p. 47).

SITUATING ELECTRONIC OUTLINING IN THE SPECTRUM OF COLLABORATIVE WORK

My enthusiasm for electronic outlining is based on my experience as a professional writer collaborating intensively on some 20 projects in technical communication over the last 10 years. To lay the groundwork for my description of the way this software can help writers in the workplace and classroom, I need to go back a decade, to explain how I came to see outlining software as such a useful tool for collaboration, through my work in industry.

Working with one to five collaborators[1] from 1984 through 1999, I used outlining software to create five manuals and six online help systems for computer companies such as Apple, Claris, Epson, and GO, dozens of workshops for teams of professional writers at major hardware and software companies, as well as 12 mostly technical books with regular publishers. The decision to use outlining software was somewhat "over-determined," as Apple (1986), Bell (1975), and Tuman (1992), have suggested is so often the case with choice of tools; one outliner had been heavily funded by a company I worked for, so I'd tried it out, liked it, and recommended it.

My collaborators and I spent some 60 percent of the entire schedule developing the outline far beyond the initial table of contents, the point at which many teams stop outlining (Allen, Atkinson, Morgan, Moore, & Snow, 1987). We worked together to flesh out the initial table of contents, putting in sections on new features as they arose, removing mention of options no longer part of the product, shifting procedures around as we came to understand them better, re-sequencing the explanations, and moving major sections forward and back.

1. During the first few months, the majority of our time was spent sitting together looking at the computer monitor, swapping the keyboard as one, then the other, got an idea. We argued about sequence, interpretation, emphasis, hierarchy, phrasing, and process until we reached agreement (not just acquiescence). We took the outline well past the initial document plan, so we could accommodate new understandings, new features, new marketing emphases. We also drove the outline down to the level of steps in procedures and explanations of individual commands. We were, in effect, researching and writing as we outlined.

2. We postponed doing any solo writing until more than half way through the project, because we wanted to keep our structure open to the latest news, and our own evolving ideas. We then took individual chapters home and fleshed them out, but unlike our experiences with similar writing, we now knew the subject inside out, and because we had really understood and agreed to the structure, we had almost no structural rethinking, reconsidering, or regrets to work through. The remaining writing went incredibly quickly, and our different modules, amazingly, dovetailed snugly, without the usual inconsistencies that show up when different writers draft different chapters, cooperatively.

3. When we got to the second and final drafts, we discovered that, unlike every solo or team project I have witnessed in the computer industry, the structure held up under the scrutiny of two dozen reviewers; we had no last-minute structural changes to make, and so, even during the last week before production, we were able to knock off by midnight.[2]

Such extended face-to-face collaboration goes well beyond the teamwork, reviewer feedback, informal chatting, E-mail exchanges, chapter swapping, and enforced cooperation that are often considered collaboration in industry (Couture & Rymer, 1989; Davis, 1977; Duin, 1991; Duin and Hansen, 1994; Ede & Lunsford, 1986, 1990; Faigley & Miller, 1982). We also went against a basic assumption of many computer-supported collaborative work applications, that electronic collaboration should take place with participants widely separated, at far ends of a network, in virtual communities (Barrett, 1988, 1989; Barrett & Paradis, 1989; Duin, 1991; Kiesler, Siegel, & McGuire, 1988; Mabrito, 1992; Olson & Atkins, 1990). We were unusual in that we used electronics to intensify direct human conversation. We wanted to see how far we could take writing toward the improvisatory collaboration of jazz.

More common is a writing process in which each author develops a tentative table of contents to go into the group's document design, but retains control and ownership over his or her chapter, book, or online system, while he or she diplomatically conforms to a thousand agreed-upon formats, phrasings, and spellings, gets reviewed by many other folks in different fields, revises according to team decisions, responds diplomatically to editorial suggestions, adjusts personal aesthetics to a corporate style and layout, and, very occasionally, incorporates suggestions from members of the intended audience. As I have seen in working on dozens of other documentation teams, as well as consulting with dozens more, all of these activities take writing well beyond the romantic idea of the individual poet scribbling alone in a garret. These activities transform writing into a social process. However, because each writer retains "ownership" of each module, the exchange of views often remains incomplete, despite a lot of nodding, and the resulting chapters retain individual differences in style, organization, and viewpoint.

Collaboration, then, may be thought of as existing along a continuum (compare Schneider, 1990), ranging from the most isolated author adjusting a line of iambic pentameter for an adored audience of one, through the give-and-take of regular technical and business writing, which I call cooperation, to the most intense form, in my opinion, the direct conversation of several people sitting around the same computer talking together as they try to make sense of a complex subject. At this more intense end of the spectrum, then, one loses all sense of personal ownership of a phrase, a sentence, a diagram; one can no longer harbor secret resentments and go home and "do it my way."

Such direct, conversational collaboration, we all concluded, worked best when we focused on questions of organization, allowing the details of phrasing to emerge in individual writing, based on our discussions of structure. Electronic outlining software gave us a way to consider alternate structures more quickly, thoroughly, and thoughtfully than any other tool we tried (paper, yellow stickies, white board drawings, diagramming software). Why? With a dedicated electronic outliner like MORE™, we were able to carry out many of the outlining activities that our teachers had encouraged in the past. In high school, we had tried those activities but given up after one or two outline drafts, because revising the outline on paper proved too tedious. Now for the first time we could see the value of beating on structure over and over, to temper it, refine it, purify it, and, ultimately, to make it understandable and usable for our users.

At this point, the reader who has had little experience with outlining software may be wondering what exactly one can do with it, and why I see it as different from regular word processing software. And even an experienced user may not have recognized all the activities made possible by the outlining module's features, because most technical writing textbooks mention only a few aspects, and few scholarly articles delve into the features, or the activities those options make possible. In the next chapter, I show how the software enables and encourages many of the structuring activities for which outlines were first assigned in school, making it possible for us to get the benefits our teachers hoped for, but rarely saw, when we pencilled outlines on paper. In addition, I will show how outlining software serves technical writers who must produce suites of books and menu systems for online help, CD-ROM's, and Web sites. Electronic outlining, it turns out, is an excellent tool for envisioning and creating the complex structures we must navigate in the online world.

NOTES

[1] I owe many of my ideas on collaboration to Henry Korman, my co-author in *How to Communicate Technical Information* (1993), and my partners: Elaine Pendergast, Lisa Price, Mick Renner, Adam Rochmes, and Linda Urban. I have also learned enormously from collaborating on books and articles with Steve Anderson, Weifeng Bao, Suzanne Brown, Chuck Campbell, Marty Downey, David Gillette, Nancy Hindle, John Lahr, Subhasish Mazumdar, Tom Outler, Randy Scasny, Carlene Schnabel, and Zhengang Yao. My ideas of collaboration also owe an enormous amount to Jack Jorgens, the Shakespearean scholar, Joel Katz, the photographer and designer, my fellow artists in the Westbroadway Gallery, a cooperative gallery in New York city, the many participants in the Association of Artist-Run Galleries, and my collaborators on the Wall project at Pleiades Gallery—Joellen Bard, Marilyn Belford, Ken Glickfeld, Jerry Herman, and E. S. Pearlman.

[2] Although collaborative outlining worked well for me and half a dozen other professional writers in industry over more than 10 years, I am not recommending it for everyone. Successful writers vary enormously in the amount of planning, exploration, drafting, and revision they do (Bridwell, 1980; Emig, 1971; Faigley & Witte, 1981; Flower & Hayes, 1981b; Harris, 1989; Witte, 1983, 1987). Still, the more complex the job, and the more professional the writer, the more likely some form of outlining will be involved. In 1972, McKee surveyed professional technical writers with an average of 12.2 years in industry, and found that 95% created some form of outline (topic, word, sentence) for projects of 3,000 words or more. Baker (1994), Hays (1982), McKee (1974/75), Plung (1982), and Wagner (1994) also all urge various forms of outlining (electronic or not) on business, professional, and technical writers as excellent techniques already being practiced by their peers. What I and my partners were trying to do, though, was to go farther, using outlining as a convivial tool for collaborative work.

2

How Electronic Outlining Helps Writers Turn Structuring into a Continuous Process

T he very thought of outlining makes many writers shudder. I understand the revulsion. When I was in high school and college, the paper outline often seemed an arbitrary chore, a rigid plan we had to follow even if we came up with a better idea later, a stupid rigamarole of labels and formats. Why did our teachers assign outlines so often?

Perhaps because our papers were, structurally, a mess. Our teachers may have hoped that in the process of outlining we would apply some organizing strategies, consider various possible structures, and emerge with the most coherent, effective, and convincing organization possible. Of course, many of us just wrote the paper and then cooked up a fake outline to get by, neatly avoiding getting any benefit out of all those outlines.

In the mid 1980s, with the invention of electronic outlining, the world received a tool that actually made it possible to get substantial benefits out of outlining. The electronic outliner made it easy to create and revise an intellectual structure, carrying out a wide variety of structuring activities.

In this chapter I will describe some of the features of the software that make restructuring an easier and more inviting task than it was with earlier tools, such as pen and paper or word processing software. Then I'll describe some of the organizing strategies that these features encourage. The strategies themselves are not new; in fact, they tend to follow common ways in which our minds work to understand a subject, by clarifying the structure of our own understanding. However, outlining software enables a writer to make a great many passes through the same material, using different strategies, developing deeper understanding of the subject, and thereby sharpening the articulate structure.

Finally, I'll summarize important ways in which some technical writers use outlining software to handle the challenge of organizing more information than ever before into suites of paper documentation, while, at the same time, moving even more information into online environments. Teams need to put together new tables of content and menu systems, to clarify the structure so users can navigate successfully. In the online world, teams must identify potential links by category, not just by whim, so that users can confidently anticipate and follow hypertext jumps. Outlining modules help the team develop entire Help systems and CD-ROMs, which, although large, are closed systems. And as writers guide the unending growth of a Web site, outlining software helps them develop top-level structures into which hundreds of thousands of documents can be dropped.

WHAT OUTLINING SOFTWARE DOES

Several computer programs offer writers the ability to create outlines electronically.[1] The original dedicated outliners like ThinkTank™, Freestyle™, MaxThink™, MORE™, and PC-Outline™, gave way to outlining views or "modes" within word-processing applications like Microsoft Word™, Corel Word Perfect™, Ashton-Tate's Framework™, and the word-processing module within the integrated package called Claris-Works™ (now called AppleWorks™), in presentation packages like Power-Point™ and Ovation™, in personal information managers such as Acta™, BrainForest™, Grandview™, and Outliner™, in idea processors such as Inspiration™ and Three-by-Five™, in Addison-Wesley's Speech Writer's Workshop Speech Outlining Software™, and in complex document processors such as Folio™, Frontier™, Dynatext™, and FrameMaker+ SGML™. In such applications, electronic outlining offers a structural perspective on the document (whether it is a report, manual, speech, or hypertext). This view supplements the formatting perspective such as Word's Page Layout view; the running text view in which many writers work word by word on style, such as Word's Normal view; and the Online Layout (or hypertext) view, in which the writer can see animated text, and active Hypertext Markup Language (HTML) links. Today's writers are fortunate to have so many ways of looking at a developing document—none of which were available so quickly, cleanly, and conveniently back when they worked solely on paper.

Electronic outlining does for the outline what word processing has done for the written draft (Crawford, 1989; Daiute, 1985; Rogers, 1986). Word processing has gradually transformed our understanding of writing, demonstrating our tendency to switch rapidly back and forth among activities such as brainstorming, note-taking, writing, or organizing. By making text easy to revise, word processing made visible what had been obscured by several decades of teachers—that real writers often revise as they go, that only a small percentage of writers know in advance exactly what they plan to say, that many folks have to go back to the subject matter expert or library to expand on a point in the middle of their writing, and that most of us cycle through all these activities repeatedly in the larger process known as writing.

Similarly, electronic outlining makes visible many activities involved in organizing verbal material, because the software makes revising the organization much easier than it would be in a traditional word-processing application, and transforms the experience dramatically, when compared to those pen-and-paper or typewritten outlines that some of us had to turn in, back in school. "Nothing remains rigidly fixed," Heim (1993) remarks of electronic outlining: "Order itself is at your disposal" (p. 49). Compared to ink and paper, the software tool offers advantages like those of a word processing application, such as

- The ability to make rapid insertions, moves, and deletions without having to redo the rest of the outline to see how the new additions fit;
- Full formatting on screen and on paper;
- Consistent indentation; and
- The ability to have styles applied automatically to format material.

However, even though the outlining software includes many of the features of word processing software, outliners include special extra features, and adaptations of others, to focus on structure. Here are some of the special capabilities of outlining software:

- The writer can single out and display all the items at the top level of the hierarchy, ignoring everything else in the document, to consider whether the sequence of major topics makes sense. (The other headings and text are temporarily "hidden," that is, not displayed.)
- At a click, the writer can reveal the subheads under a major heading, while hiding everything below them, to consider the sequence of subheads without being distracted by intervening text. The writer can also compare them with the overarching topic to ensure that it adequately expresses the information in its section.

- The writer can hide and reveal the running text under any heading, just by clicking. If the writer wants to compare the contents of two heads, the writer can open both, and compare, without any intervening text, scrolling, or searching. The writer gets to explore content by pointing and clicking.
- The writer can lift out an entire section, pulling it out of its context to work on it in isolation, ignoring everything else during that analysis and revision, then drop it back into place. This process is sometimes known as hoisting, and de-hoisting.
- The writer can also have the outline open to reveal, say, the first four levels of headings, but nothing below; or just the top level; or all the levels within a particular section, but no other. In this way the writer can shift the scale at which he or she views the material, leaping from a bird's eye view to a worm's eye view, and back, while thinking about the structure.
- The writer can easily move an entire section by dragging its heading, without any cutting or pasting, and without any reformatting. (The outliner reformats the entire topic in the style assigned to that particular level, in that section.) Using this easy move, a writer can sort a whole list of topics into bins, or categories, creating a two-level organization out of a simple list—a first crack at organizing after brainstorming. Moving also lets a writer test a topic out in different locations, to discover where it really fits best.
- The writer can take a topic that originally rambled through several subjects, and divide that into distinct topics by some simple action such as pressing Enter after the first subject. This feature helps the writer break apart a single topic. The reverse is possible, too; with a single backspace, two topics can be joined together. Notice that the thinking—and therefore the actions allowed—revolve around distinct topics, as chunks, rather than a continuously flowing text.
- Instead of having to remember an arbitrary labeling system based on capitalization of the English alphabet and use of the Roman number system, the writer can assign each level its own format, or style. That way, whenever the writer creates a new topic at a certain level, it inherits the level's style, too. A reader can see immediately where it fits into the hierarchy. Similarly, when the writer drags a topic to that level, its style automatically changes, to reflect its new position in the hierarchy. Multiple cues indicate level and dependency: The traditional left-right and up-down positioning and typographical labels are supplemented with color, size, font, slant, and emphasis, as well as line spacing, and spacing between topics. (If a writer still likes labels ahead of each topic, the software can insert those automatically, so the numbering is always correct.)

- The writer can record notes within the evolving structure, writing whole paragraphs at a low level, hiding them to look at structure, and revealing them to reread, think about them, plan, or write. Note-taking, then, fits right into the outline, as does writing. The same electronic document accommodates all three activities.

- The writer can create an entire document in the same file as the outline, simply switching from outline view to text view, returning to the outline view when considering questions of structure. In this way, the outline is always in sync with the written document. Thus, the writer can always show and hide text, to examine headings in relation to text and in relation to each other, and redo headings or text over and over, whereas a paper outline is soon outdated.

Overall, then, analyzing and revising structure becomes much easier with the outlining software than with regular word processing software (Burnor, 1995). However, many people who have not used electronic outlining believe that they could get similar results just by cutting and pasting in their table of contents. Such revisions do allow reordering of a table of contents, but when a writer is just working in the table of contents, the relevant text is not visible without some scrolling, or opening a separate file (whereas the outlining software, at a click, shows the related text, or hides it). Similarly, cutting and pasting in a word processing view means that a writer does get a new organization, but must go to considerable extra effort to change the format of the headings so that after each revision, the headings at each level take on their own look—a big help when studying and revising the structure. Essentially, the word processing software is built on a model of running text, flowing on and on, whereas the outlining software envisions an indented hierarchy, with all the text tucked into memory, ready to be shown for review, then hidden to get it out of the way for further exploration of the organization. Automatic formatting of a topic whenever it lands at a certain level also eliminates the extra work needed in word processing, where the writer has to select the entire topic, strip it of its previous formatting, then apply the correct new style, all of which distracts from the original thinking about structural relationships. Seeing each level in its own format, with indents, colors, fonts, sizes, even emphasis applied automatically as an item drops into that level, speeds up recognition of the difference between one topic and another, and enables continued focus on the questions of organization.

The special features of outlining software allow writers to carry on analysis, experimentation, comparison, and revision of the arrangement much longer than anyone could stand doing with a series of paper outlines. Outlining software, then, offers us a structural view—the very term used in Word, where Outline is an option on the View menu, and in PowerPoint®, where the Outline View lets one look at the text of the slides arranged hierarchically and sequentially without the art, so one can switch back and forth between the images an audience will see and the ideas one is trying to convey verbally. Electronic outlining, in whatever form, helps us to think structurally, and to keep on thinking that way as we learn new material.

EXPANDING THE ORGANIZING PROCESS

The special features of outlining software allow the writer to cycle through a variety of organizing strategies more aggressively, and more often, than seemed possible when using paper. Some of these strategies can be done perfectly well in other views (such as Page Layout or Normal, in Word), but all of them can be done in the Outline view, so writers can switch from one strategy to another without having to change views. And some of these strategies can only be done quickly in the outlining software, because of its dedication to issues of structure. The strategies of organization include:

- Identifying all potential topics in a list, no matter what level they will end up at;
- Moving topics around;
- Adding or deleting topics;
- Annotating topics;
- Eliminating duplicate or redundant topics;
- Dividing one topic into its components;
- Creating a new topic out of the details;
- Disassembling a set of subtopics;
- Promoting a subtopic or demoting a topic;
- Grouping;
- Sequencing topics;
- Rewriting to emphasize similarity and difference;
- Rewriting to reveal the structure;
- Writing test passages, even final drafts of sections;
- Verifying that similar topics have similar subtopics; and
- Confirming completeness.

By making all of these strategies more convenient, the software encourages the writer to extend and deepen the process of arrangement, because one strategy often turns up problems that require another approach, and that in turns requires a third strategy, in some other location. For the audience, the resulting outline is noticeably more effective than the one-shot table of contents of traditional document design (Korman & Price, 1993) or lecture notes (Burnor, 1995). Burnor, reflecting on the results of using an outliner to prepare philosophy lectures, says, "I have noted (i) a significant gain in the ease with which students follow even difficult material, (ii) a sizable increase in the amount of material I can effectively cover in a set period of time, and (iii) a noticeable reduction in class time spent on tangential discussion" (Teaching Preparation, n.p.)

Being able to keep working the structure as new information appears, on every level, helps the writer avoid freezing the organization while it may still be incomplete, only partially accurate, or slightly ambiguous. At some point the writer must send the outline off for review or publication, so there is always a "product," but it is, in this situation, more of a snapshot of the current state of the writer's thinking than a blueprint drawn up months before, and followed slavishly despite changes in the audience, the subject matter, or the writer's own understanding—as in the traditional idea of an outline.

The strategies for organizing topics are not new, but as we will see in Chapter 4, the paper medium seems to have discouraged writers from pursuing any of these strategies for long. Imagine, as you browse through this list of activities, the writer applying each strategy to every level, and almost every section. Outlining software makes it easy for the writer to pursue these interrelated strategies repeatedly, persistently, and deeply.

Identifying all Potential Topics in a List, No Matter What Level They Will End Up At

Because the software makes moving topics easy, writers seem unafraid of brainstorming an unordered list, just to get the topics down before they are forgotten. Such preliminary thinking often includes some rudimentary structuring activities (grouping, sequencing, subordinating), made easier by the outlining software, which lets the writer change a whole topic's position by dragging and dropping (rather than erasing and rewriting on paper, or cutting and pasting in a word processing program). Brainstorming often advances with a burst of ideas, followed by a period of reorganization, then more random ideas. Like word processing software, the outlining modules make listing easy; unlike word processing software, though, the outlining module encourages reordering.

Moving Topics Around

The simplest restructuring involves dragging topics up or down in the list, to new locations, following some rough-and-ready reasoning such as,

"These belong together," or, "You have to have done this in order to do that," or "Aren't these related, somehow?"

Adding or Deleting Topics

As writers start looking at the list they have brainstormed and begun to reorder, they often recognize items they forgot to add, or weak versions of those, and begin adding and deleting topics. Inserting a new topic simply pushes following topics down; deleting means other topics move up to fill the gap. From moment to moment, the list looks "final," even though it is always open.

Annotating Topics

Individual topics can be enriched with comments, rough drafts of sentences, paragraphs, and footnotes, as research proceeds (explaining and expanding on what the heading means). Because these notes are easily hidden, they do not interfere with comparisons between headings, but when their heading is called into question, the notes can be revealed, to determine whether the heading really reflects the gist of the information.

Eliminating Duplicate or Redundant Topics

This strategy clears away the debris of brainstorming—synonyms and different terms for the same subject can be relegated to notes; two closely related topics can be merged into one; and when several phrases that sound similar turn out to refer to very different subjects, the headings can be rewritten to reflect the distinction. Writers seem to assume an economy of attention, figuring that most readers will expect a given topic to be dealt with only once, and then, if necessary, referred back to. This apparently simple activity often forces the writers to do more research, exploring the difference between two topics, and returning with that information to revise the actual phrasing of headings. Intellectually, this process helps the writers define what is, and what is not, the same—a key step toward genuine understanding of the material.

Example: In one class, we considered these three topics that had emerged from a brainstorming session: "Status messages, Feedback, Error Messages." Rereading the specifications and the manual, we concluded that the only feedback from the software (other than a complete system crash) involved these two kinds of messages. So we could eliminate the Feedback topic, as redundant with the Messages. And as we compared the descriptions of various messages, we learned that there was only one Status message, a count-down indicating how much longer the processing would take. But, there were dozens of error messages, all distinct from this little ticker. So we ended up with a status message (singular) and error messages. Upon further discussion, we concluded that really what people might want to know was the status of their job, so instead of calling this a message, we used the title "Status Information." Resulting topics: "Status Information, Error Messages." Undertaking the apparently trivial activity of removing duplicates can require new research, driving slight but meaningful rewrites.

Dividing One Topic into its Components

As writers record more information about a topic, they may begin to recognize that the subject has a number of phases, components, options, features, benefits, or themes, described in the text hidden beneath the heading. To reflect this understanding the writers may break the text up into subtopics (for instance, by pressing Enter before each one) or create a new set of subtopics underneath the original, parceling passages of text out among them by dragging, or copying and pasting. As soon as an item becomes a subtopic, it takes on the style of that level, automatically. Division works well with subjects such as dialog boxes, where the writers may want to list each option as a subtopic, but not everything can be neatly divided into components. For instance, some steps in a procedure need explanations and illustrations, and others don't. Some commands take 30 arguments, and others none. The outlining software lets the writers quickly create a test set of subtopics (formatted correctly) to consider whether they are all truly components of the major topic.

Creating a New Topic out of the Details

Occasionally writers notice that they have touched glancingly on the same subject in different sections, perhaps taking a different look at it, perhaps discussing a different aspect, or component. When writers spot topics that may be related, they ask whether the different texts answer different questions from the audience, in which case the answers may really be distinct subtopics. If the different texts seem to answer the same question, though, perhaps one can be cut. Writers also ask themselves: If they were to bring these various low-level topics together, what category would have to be created to contain them, and how much meaning would be added to the topics by placing them close together? This activity of assembling various low-level topics under a new higher-level topic allows writers to synthesize and unify material that would otherwise be disturbingly distributed across the hierarchy.

Disassembling a Set of Subtopics

Sometimes the first approach to organizing breaks down, as writers learn more about the subject or the audience. For instance, in documenting a personnel program for clerks, one team started out organizing its information about adding a new employee to the database with actions (adding, editing, archiving). But further interviews with the data-entry clerks revealed that they thought about objects first, and actions second, so the team had to revise the hierarchy to put objects at the top level (Personnel Record, Salary Record, so on), and only under those to include actions (Adding a Personnel Record, Editing a Personnel Record, Archiving a Personnel Record). Disassembling one group of subtopics and distributing them among other topics often means building up new groups. The electronic outlining software makes such changes as simple as dragging and dropping the topics in their new locations in the hierarchy.

Promoting a Subtopic or Demoting a Topic

In revising any rough list of topics, writers impose a hierarchical arrangement on it by promoting one topic or demoting another—that is, turning a low-level item into something at a higher level, or, contrarywise, turning a major topic into a subtopic under another subject. Intellectually, the writers are asking questions such as:

- Do all of these subtopics really belong under this topic? (Is it a step within another procedure, rather than a separate procedure? An option under a command, rather than a command? Background for one of the other topics, rather than a topic on its own?)
- Does this topic actually subsume any other topics we now have at the same level?

In this way, writers are dealing with the scale of individual topics, debating whether every item at a particular height in the hierarchy really belongs at that level. Pondering the question, writers have to reexamine the information they have about the subject, considering its position in the hierarchy from different perspectives, such as the team's sense of the topic's importance, the audience's expectations about the topic, and the valuations placed on the topic by source material, peers, and test participants. For instance writers may realize that a topic they had originally put low in the hierarchy because it contains little material, should be promoted, because it is critical for the user. (Quitting, for instance, is an important procedure even though it only contains one step). Like a juggler tossing more and more balls in the air, collaborators often find their minds entertaining many considerations, and any decision, whether to promote, demote, or leave in place, results from intricate negotiation in their minds and in conversations with each other. Being able to move a topic up and down lets every member of the team contemplate alternate hierarchies without the distractions of word-processing's cutting, pasting, and formatting.

Grouping

Whenever writers find a set of topics at the same level, under the same topic, they face the strategic question: In what order should these topics appear? One approach to organizing the set of topics involves grouping subsets around similar activities, objects, or attributes. For instance, in a set of procedures about drawing electrical components, there may be three dealing with the power supply; those might be grouped together, as a start at organization, particularly if three other topics deal with connectors, and three more with wiring. By dragging together the topics with some common attribute, to form small subgroups, writers may enable the user to compare them more easily, seeing how they resemble each other, and differ.

Sequencing Topics

Even when they have created subgroups, bringing together several of the topics at the same level, under the same topic, writers may still face questions of sequence for the whole set. In many textbooks, the authors suggest that "logic" will dictate the order of topics, but when we look more closely and ask how logic does this, we find that the authors generally just mean that we should resort to some common-sensical pattern of thought such as chronological or geographical order, or progression from cause to effect, problem to solution, familiar to unfamiliar, important to unimportant, common to rare, or feature to benefit. Users trying to understand our organization will often look for one of these patterns, expecting, for example, a chronological sequence for time-based topics such as procedures. Spotting such a pattern in the headings confirms the user's mental map of the material, and gives the user confidence to explore it in more depth. With complex subjects, not so open to instant patterning, writers are forced to start with a dominant pattern, then use other patterns to fill in the gaps. For instance, one writer might put familiar items first, and totally unfamiliar items last, but have to organize the in-between items in some other way, such as starting with the more commonly used, and going to the less commonly used. Deciding the sequence of five, ten, twenty different items often requires doing additional research, and once writers do decide on a pattern, they may have to rewrite some headings to show the plan more clearly. Throughout, the ease with which one can drag topics up and down allows writers to experiment with different orders, through direct manipulation, rather than having to build castles in air, or cut and paste endlessly.

Rewriting to Emphasize Similarity and Difference

Eventually, users will consult a table of contents or menu (that is, the final version of the outline of headings) to locate information, making a series of comparisons between the headings. To make this comparison easier, writers may decide to phrase all procedure headings in the same grammatical format (such as –ing phrases); in that way, the actual phrasing of the headings—the style, if you will—telegraphs that each contains a procedure. Similarly, if writers consistently phrase all conceptual overviews in a different grammatical form, users learn to distinguish these headings from headings for procedures, avoiding potential mistakes in menu choices. For instance, having created a number of –ing phrases for procedures describing how to create a form letter, one team eventually realized they had to explain what a form letter was, and added a topic, "About Form Letters." The difference in phrasing, the team hoped, would indicate that this topic contained no step-by-step instructions, so the impatient could avoid it, while the truly confused would visit here first.

Formulaic as it is, this kind of rewriting is the first of many edits needed to make the actual writing of the headings reflect the reasoning behind the organization. By hiding intervening text, the electronic outliner makes the need for rewriting menu items more visible than a word processor could, and the edits themselves can be done just as easily as in a word processor.

This kind of rewriting resembles the only writing the textbooks recognize as necessary in an outline, that is, expressing all the subtopics under one topic in the same form (Elsbree & Bracher, 1967, p. 40; Jordan, 1965, p. 109; Leggett, Mead, & Charvat, 1960, p. 201; Pickett & Laster, 1984, p. 118; Shelton, 1995, p. 41; Sherman, 1955, p. 14; Sypherd, Fountain, & Gibbens, 1957, p. 144). The textbook rationales differ, but include the following: All components of the same category should logically be in the same form, all headings at the same level and position in the hierarchy ought to be parallel, consistency of format allows faster and more accurate comparison by the reader, consistency of form emphasizes whatever principle the items have in common. In technical writing, though, we often need to perform several functions in the same section, introducing a group of procedures, explaining key concepts, providing procedures, and offering a summary, for instance, and so not every subhead ought to get the same format.

Rewriting to Reveal the Structure

Often, when writers have rearranged topics in a new order, they discover that they need to make editorial changes to the individual headings, to show why one appears before another, and what one heading has in common with another, quite aside from ensuring parallelism among headings for material serving the same function. For instance, if a writer has chosen a chronological order for the items, she might rewrite the first topic to show that she put it first because the user has to do it before any other tasks, changing the language from "Using the Rambler Library" to "Opening the Library to Start Rambler." These little edits, carried through the entire outline, make the relationships between items at the same level (and between topic and subtopics) clearer to the user. By hiding subordinate text, the outlining software makes it easy for writers to compare the headings, and to rewrite while keeping our eye on the effect on the set, or menu, as a whole.

Writing Test Passages, Even Final Drafts of Sections

As writers develop understanding of a particular topic, they may write the actual text they expect to put in their final document. Running text, in an outline view, is simply material at a very low level, and writers can open and close the passage, if they need to go elsewhere in the document to check a fact, or make sure they haven't already discussed a topic. The ability to move through the document as a menu system makes the writing process go forward with fewer delays, because writers can always check what they have written elsewhere, without getting lost in scrolling, or a blur of text.

Verifying that Similar Topics Have Similar Subtopics

With a developed outline, writers may want to make sure they haven't inadvertently left sections out. One way to check is to open each topic that serves the same function, to make sure that each has the same kind of components. The outliner makes it easy to open and hide one topic after another, in this way, for quick comparison.

Confirming Completeness

In a long document, writers can easily leave something out. Looking at pages and pages of text scrolling past in a word processor's normal view, a writer can't easily check for a missing element. On the other hand, the outlining software lets the writer skim and skip through the material, going up and down through the hierarchy, to check the emerging outline against the research materials, making sure that no significant topic has been left out.

How Strategies Overlap

These strategies do not operate in isolation. Starting to apply one strategy in one area frequently leads to further research, discussion, and questions that drive writers to try another strategy in some other area, in order to clarify some idea on which the first strategy ran aground. Attention moves from a top-level overview to a low-level detail, from first to second to third in a sequence, and back. Encouraged by the convenience of the tool, writers may find themselves making many passes through every niche of the structure, perfecting it at every level, through a constellation of strategies.

As writers apply all these strategies, the electronic outliner serves as a tool for thinking. The thinking can be described as ordinary, that is, following common patterns of thought—ones that the writers hope their readers will recognize. Burnor (1995) argues that outlining helps students analyze themes and logical structures:

> To outline a sustained argument, for instance, one first identifies each of the several subarguments offered in support of the proponent's final conclusion; one then identifies the explicit and implicit premises constituting each of these arguments, with further justificatory and/or critical remarks included as subtopics of each distinct premise. Counter-examples, objections, and responses can also be appropriately positioned so as to further elucidate what might constitute a complex and difficult train of thought. Finally, conceptual relationships may also be portrayed via the outline format: in explicating the conceptual structure of a theory, for example, one can effectively illustrate the hierarchical relationships between fundamental, subsidiary, and derived concepts and terms by means of an outline." (The Outline as a Learning Tool)

Heim (1993) agrees, saying the "outlining is basic thinking" (p. 46), but going farther to stress that the fluidity and ease of change mirrors the movement of mind, as it interacts with its own most recent artifact. He calls electronic outlining a form of idea processing or thought processing, in a form unknown in school exercises and modern printed texts.

At the grammar school level, the U.S. Department of Education (1997) has recommended electronic outlining as a tool to help children with disabilities "collect and comprehend large volumes of information" (Assembling Complex Information), as in preparing a research report. The activities of electronic outlining, then, seem to reflect and facilitate many kinds of thinking, from simple grouping to complex hierarchies.

Thinking involves testing out various models, and reworking the components. Like a Lego™ kit, the pieces of the outline can be reassembled in many different ways, allowing the writers to consider the rhetorical impact of each new structure, and then, without losing track of that, to ponder the effectiveness of an alternate structure. DeKoven (1998b), who uses outlining software to facilitate meetings, stresses the malleability and changeability of the material: "With electric print, we can work with different ideas like sculptors, molding them together into a single statement, allowing them to be in formation until we can form them into information. We can maintain a greater diversity of opinions, and, when we need to, cut and paste, drag and drop, point and click them into a single vision" (n. p.). By externalizing their own thoughts, writers can interrogate them. In effect, through this kind of bricolage, writers carry on a conversation with their thought of just a minute ago.

This process, when carried out week after week during a developing project, means that writers often bump into many of the problems with their earlier organizations. They learn as they go, and revise the structure to reflect their deeper knowledge. The outline, like the document, remains open, growing. As Heim (1993) says, "Traditional outlines on paper are immovable. You do not interact with them. If you want to make additions or changes in hierarchy, you have to redo the entire outline or a good part of it. Electronic outliners are infinitely more flexible ... " (p. 48).

This openness contrasts dramatically with the textbooks' traditional school model, which conceives of writers locating a number of "facts" through research, applying something called "logic" to those facts, and then recording the "thoughts" that emerged in an outline, to serve as a static blueprint for the document that will be built mainly by "expanding" on those thoughts in the draft (Alvarez, 1980, p. 157; Brusaw, Alred,.& Oliu, 1993, p. 485; Damerst, 1982, p. 59; Dietrich & Brooks, 1958, 109-111; Elsbree & Bracher, 1967, p. 39; Fowler, Aaron, & Limburg, 1992, p. 39; Hacker, 1994, p. 46; Hacker & Renshaw, 1979, p. 107; Harwell, 1960, pp.122-3; Hays, 1965, p. 104; Johnson, 1992, p. 141; Jordan, 1965, pp. 108-111; Leggett et al., 1960, pp. 196-7; Lester, 1990, p. 114; Marckwardt & Cassidy, 1960, p. 408; Markel, 1984, p. 70; Mills & Walter, 1962, p.45; Rubens, 1992, p. 15; Shelton, 1995, p. 42; Sherman, 1955, p. 12, and 1966, p. 34; Smart & Lang, 1943, pp. 19-26; Thomas, 1949, pp. 130-142; Weiss, 1982, p. 52 ; Wellborn, Green, & Nall, 1961, p. 55; Wicker & Albrecht, 1960, p. 54; Wilcox, 1977, p. 83-86.).

Now, in electronic outlining, these activities overlap, so outlining takes place alongside research, brainstorming, and writing. As Heim (1993) summarizes, "Outlining becomes a creative environment in which thinking, writing, and planning coexist in an outlined structure. Unlike modern outlines, outliners do not merely schematize a passively received volume of knowledge. Rather, the postmodern outliner is a working environment in which you strive constantly to think in order to produce" (p. 50). A few examples of these overlapping activities:

- If a topic appears empty, the writer goes back to the source for more information, brings that back in the form of a note, or extra subtopics, or a paragraph—or deletes the whole topic.
- If two topics seem similar, but ambiguous, the writer goes back to the source for more information, then returns, and merges them, or rewrites one to distinguish it more clearly.
- If the writer finds that a minor subtopic is turning into eight pages, the outline view allows it to be moved up a notch, to indicate a new awareness of its importance.
- New ideas can be dropped into the outline, as placeholders, waiting to be fleshed out later.

Thus, electronic outlining allows structuring to take its full place as part of the whole process of creating meaningful information, a process we used to call writing.

Formatting itself may be considered another intellectual strategy involved in designing the evolving structure. Using a different style (font, size, color, indent, so on) for each level certainly helps clarify and reveal the structure, making it easier to manipulate (Apple Computer, 1987; Hutchins, Hollan, & Norman, 1986; Shneiderman, 1983, 1992; Young, 1991). The outlining software enables the writer to make one decision about the format of each level, ahead of time, and have that applied automatically from then on—allowing the writer to focus on structure, not the often annoying effort to reformat. Writers no longer have to spend as much effort on labeling (I, II, IIa, IIb, and so on) as they did in the paper world. No one faces a tangle of crossouts and overlays when making changes, as on paper. And because the outliner applies the format to a topic as soon as it appears at a particular level, writers avoid the tedious reformatting and labeling they would have to do in a word processor.. The interweaving of text and design available in word processors has been well described by Bernhardt (1986), Costanzo (1994), Hawisher (1991), Kaplan and Moulthrop (1993), Kostelnick (1989b, 1990, 1994, 1996), Landow and Delany (1993), Lanham (1993), Rude (1988), and Ruskiewicz (1988). But that process, appropriate for the formatting of running text, becomes tedious when the writer is making frequent and major changes to an indented hierarchy. In the outlining software, after every change writers have a clean outline, ready for further study and work (Heim, 1993).

In this sense, outlining software extends the graphic nature of electronic writing, allowing the creator to more fully "exploit the spatial and visual dimensions of texts," as Kaplan and Moulthrop (1993, p. 265) remark. Bolter (1991) points out that:

> Electronic writing is both a visual and verbal description. It is not the writing of a place, but rather a writing with places, spatially realized topics. Topographic writing challenges the idea that writing should be merely the servant of spoken language. The writer and reader can create and examine signs and structures on the computer screen that have no easy equivalent in speech. (p. 25)

Lanham (1993) talks of toggling back and forth between visual and verbal syntax on the screen (p. 77), but in the electronic outliner, these syntaxes work together, instantaneously reenforcing each other. In this sense, the automated graphic formatting offered by electronic outlining helps articulate the moment-to-moment structure that is being built out of the writer's ongoing notetaking, thinking, and drafting.

HOW ELECTRONIC OUTLINING HELPS TECHNICAL WRITERS

Many technical writers intuitively carry out these activities of structural analysis, construction, and reconstruction when making up a table of contents as part of a document design. But once that design is approved, teams often work within that structure as a given, and write to justify it, even when the individual writers begin to sense that there are some problems. (Often these problems blow up in their faces at the beta review meeting, when there is very little time to solve them).

By making it easy to continue and expand the work we put into structure, outlining software helps us improve the quality of material destined for paper or the screen—for books and suites of books, for fixed menu systems like those for help facilities or CD-ROMs, and for constantly expanding online information environments such as intranets, extranets, and general Web sites. The more information we face, the more we need this kind of structuring, to organize it, retrieve parts of it, update other parts, and expand as new information comes in.

Making Libraries

Switching from normal word processing to the outlining view allows technical writers to create more effective structures for large, complex documents such as books, suites of books, or libraries containing multiple suites, a common index, and a unified table of contents. In creating an encyclopedia-like reference, a thousand-page proposal, documentation for a software developer's kit, or even a set of manuals for an enterprise-wide database, the wise technical writer keeps the outline going well into the project, adjusting the structure as the specifications change, features come and go, user interface elements are renamed and repositioned, and whole modules get incorporated, even when they don't mesh with the rest of the material. Using outlining software to re-examine the structure on a continuing basis lets the writer perform the kind of study and redesign traditionally performed by a developmental editor, who focused on the large rhetorical question, Is this organization meeting the needs of the reader? But where the developmental editor may have made one or two passes, resulting in a "final," agreed-upon outline that the writer would follow, the writer who uses outlining software can, in effect, perform dozens, even hundreds, of editorial reviews while incorporating changes imposed by a fluid project team or morphing subject matter. Going well beyond the initial outline that most writers settle for, this continuously changing outline helps individual writers and teams eliminate the annoying inconsistencies, ambiguities, and chaos that creep into most books, suites, and libraries, because of the way they are written—one chapter at a time, with the head bent low over that particular subject, ignoring any impacts on other sections. The plunge into writing generally means the writer becomes wrapped up in one section, and forgets or ignores the content and structure of sections that lead up to this one, follow it, or resemble it. In brief, the extended work on structure encouraged by outlining software helps eliminate problems that readers often encounter, such as:

- Chapter titles that sound confusingly alike, making the reader wonder which to pick.
- Chapter tables of contents that do not match the main table of contents, or the actual sequence of headings within the chapter, making the reader wonder which to use.
- Headings that do not reveal the content of their sections clearly enough for a reader to decide whether or not to read on.
- Headings that mislead the reader about the type of section they announce (overviews that are not, how-to's that involve no actions, concept sections that focus on step-by-step procedures).

- Several sections whose headings sound alike and evidently deal with the same type of subject, but that turn out to be organized in completely different ways, confusing the reader who got accustomed to the first organization and wonders if there is some significance to the change (or, worse, invents a fantastical explanation for the difference).
- Similar topics appearing at very different levels (with, say, Number One heads in one section, and Number Four heads in another) raising the question: Are they really similar?
- The same basic topic (described in three different terms) appearing in several different chapters, or in different books (but explained differently by various authors) raising the question: which is correct?
- Several sections that seem to deal with the same topic, but don't
- Flow diagrams that use modules not referred to in the subsequent headings or text, or show modules in an order not reflected in the text, leading the reader to wonder: which sequence is right?
- Procedures that do not appear in chronological order (quitting before editing)
- Topographical tours that do not follow any recognizable geographical pattern
- Command references that pile subtopics into a single paragraph, in no set order, and therefore often leave out or bury the precise piece of information the reader wants.
- Cross references that fail.
- Introductions that leave out key topics covered in the section, or announce all the topics, but not in the order they are presented, so the reader starts with an incorrect map of the material.
- Comparisons that discuss the first issue at length, and forget the other.
- Bulleted lists that announce several topics, followed by sections that only cover one or two of them, leading readers to wonder if they are losing their minds.

Such immature structures are, almost by accident, incomplete, inaccurate, and ambiguous. They confuse readers, frustrating their attempts to form a mental model of the material (a model that is itself a structure), baffling their attempts to locate information, and arousing those emotions we feel so often when using technical documents—anger mixed with self-doubt. No one of these problems defeats a determined reader, but taken as a group, a series of interrelated messes can force the reader to give up using a book or set.

Outlining software, by itself, offers no guarantee of good thinking. But, on large projects, where no one human being can recall all the details at any one time, the software encourages continuous investigation of the structure, as it evolves—more passes through the hierarchy, more explorations and comparisons, more experiments, as the writer struggles to find the organization that can most efficiently serve these readers. Short documents such as quick references or college essays rarely require the writer to keep a lot of topics in the foreground of the mind, so they do not need a lot of outlining; but books, and whole sets of books, can benefit enormously from this extended structural work.

Making Menus

Imagine the challenge of putting 2,000 documents from eight different divisions into a single online information system. The writers are looking at a larger and more complex table of contents than they ever saw in a book, suite, or library. Then their boss tells them that they have to present all those documents on the organization's Web site, and while they are at it, could they add 500 application notes, 100 documents answering frequently asked questions, all the press releases from the last year, and the annual report? What does the table of contents, or menu system, look like now?

As the volume of information increases, not just arithmetically, but exponentially (NUA Internet Surveys, 1998; Larson, 1996), writers must pay more attention to creating meaningful menu systems, reflecting huge structures of information (Mazumdar et al., 1998; Price, 1997a, 1997b, 1997c). Trying to capture this new role that unites writerly, interface, and design skills, Cook (1996), Nielsen (1999), and Wurman (1996) have popularized the term *Information Architect*, which the designer Wurman defines as "1) the individual who organizes the patterns inherent in data, making the complex clear, 2) a person who creates the structure or map of information which allows others to find their personal paths to knowledge" (cover). Struggling with the same expansion of roles, Mok (1996) says, "Each of the information arts is a craft on which the practice of information design is built. Information architecture is the integration of the structures underlying a system" (p. 98). Schriver (1997) urges the term "document designer" to cover both traditional technical communication and this new expansion into the World Wide Web. Within the Society for Technical Communication (1998), a special interest group in Information Design has been growing very rapidly during the last few years, while practitioners argue at length on the InfoDesign list (1998) as to exactly what term describes the work that has been done, and the similar work that seems to be exploding exponentially on the Web. Rosenfeld and Morville (1998) use the term *Information Architecture* as the title for their book on organizing information and creating appropriate labels, interface systems, and search mechanisms. They describe the challenge faced by technical communicators who have to create entire Web sites:

> The process of content mapping involves breaking down or combining existing documents into logical content components or chunks, thereby separating the content from its container. A content chunk is not a sentence or a paragraph or a page. Rather, it is the most finely grained portion of content that merits or requires individual treatment. The content, often received from a variety of sources and in a multitude of formats, must be mapped onto the information architecture. (p.165)

In their book on web design, Horton, Taylor, Ignacio, and Holt (1996) suggest dozens of cluster structures, to suit various writers' purposes. But individual teams will probably have to create even more structural patterns, which users will encounter as a series of menus, whether they look like a book's tables of contents, pulldown menus, tables with rows and columns, maps, or hot images.

Because it can so effectively display topics in lists like those in the final menus, the electronic outliner lets writers analyze and improve their menus at every level, giving quick answers to questions such as:

- What is the top-level menu that greets newcomers to the Web site?
- How many levels exist in the deepest section of the material?
- Can more topics be moved up to the higher level menus, so the help system grows wide and shallow, and users don't have to make more than half a dozen decisions to reach significant content?
- Down at the third level, in this particular subtopic, what menu should be presented to users?
- On one particular menu, isolated from all others, can users tell the difference between individual topics, and recognize the reasoning behind the sequence, at least partially?

The electronic outliner also helps writers modify menus to respond to the demands of their user interface czar. For instance, menus in a graphic user interface are supposed to help users recognize the action they want to take, rather than remember a weird command, but the user should not have to recall what was on a previous menu in order to understand what is on the menu now visible—a common problem, as Mandel (1996) points out (p. 154). By isolating the menu in an outliner, writers can rewrite the items so the menu stands on its own, without depending on the users knowing what topic they chose earlier. Similarly, to keep from blowing people's short-term memory, many user-interface folks request that writers separate a longish menu into smaller groups (less than 7 items each, as in Mandel, 1996, p. 154). Using the outliner, writers can experiment with various possible groupings, tinkering until they fit (and, hopefully, make sense).

A single interface may accommodate graphic, verbal, push-button, radio-button, check-box, pull-down, pop-up, and cascading menus. Writers need to decide which kind of menu to use at each level. Once they have decided the type of menu to use at, say, the fourth level, the writers may need to go back and rewrite those particular headings so they work in that environment. For instance, the writers may need to compress the text of each topic dramatically, so it will eventually fit into a hot diagram, without losing track of the relationships between the topics. Because it displays each set of topics in isolation for study and revision, the outlining software presents writers with a preview of each menu, and the tools to improve its effectiveness.

Improving Navigation by Clarifying Structure

As users move through online information, they build a mental map of the structure. Like people walking through a city, users tend to remember the decision points better than the material in between; that is, they remember whenever they chose to make a turn (Lynch, 1960, p. 72) or, in hypertext terms, a jump. When users can recall each choice, in order, they feel secure, but most people have short-term memory capable of recalling only seven plus or minus two items (Miller, 1956). So if a team forces users to make more than five or six decisions on the trail of a fact, many users begin to lose track of the trail itself. In extreme cases, the users begin to feel disoriented and experience hypernausea.

The structure indicated by menus serves as a model for users, reassuring them that they can predict where they will go next, and that they can remember where they have been. Newcomers to a content area often find that a well-defined, conventional structure helps them decide what is important and what is not (Johnson-Eilola, 1994, p. 207; van Dijk & Kintsch, pp. 55-59). If writers write menus with as much carelessness as most book authors do their tables of contents, users may get lost (Anderson, Campbell, Hindle, Price, & Scasny, 1997). Charney (1994) summarizes extensive research when she says that readers "understand and learn most easily from texts with well-defined structures that clearly signal shifts between parts (p. 207). In fact, having a structural overview at hand during a search through the material increases recall, recognition of relations, and inferences (p. 252), but when users encounter gaps they cannot understand, they make bridging guesses, as so often happens in poorly organized hypertext environments, as described by Harpold (1991, p. 177) and Johnson-Eilola (1994, p. 212). Result: confusion. Charney

(1994) concludes: "If the goal is to ensure that readers consider a specific set of associations, then a highly organized text format is more likely to achieve that aim than an amorphous network" (p. 243). Her recommendation echoes good sense: "Thus, it is easier to read, comprehend, and remember a text if it contains an informative title, headings, overviews, and topic sentences introducing key concepts that are repeated and developed in successive portions of text" (p. 245).

If the interface allows the users to consult the outline at all times, as in Folio Views®, Guide®, or Dynatext®, then users frequently move their attention back and forth between text and outline, trying to understand why the material appears where it does, in the hierarchy. The same mental back-and-forth movement takes place even when the interface does not allow the user to view an open outline on the side, as a guide to the material. Users constantly ask themselves, "Am I in the right place? Did I reach the target I expected? Is this really what I thought it would be, or was I fooled by that last menu item?"

Handling books, users have developed many strategies for overcoming poor organization—skimming the headings, browsing the text, flipping pages looking for the next chapter. None of these strategies works well online because the low resolution, poor contrast, and small screen work together to defeat skimming and browsing, and users can't flip pages. As a result, users must rely much more heavily on headings and subheads to get a sense of location in a sequence and position in a hierarchy. The outline, translated into a menu system, bears a heavier responsibility for the user's sense of place and ability to move through your information world.

Fortunately, an electronic outliner allows a writer to examine and revise each heading in two ways: as one item in a menu, and as a heading at the top of a virtual page of material. As an item in a menu, it must stand out from the others, while advertising its content well enough so no one picks it by mistake, and anyone looking for that content spots it and chooses it right away. Then, when the user arrives at the page (frame, block, window, screen, whatever), the heading or title at the top of the page must match the menu item exactly, to confirm that the user has arrived at the right place. The first paragraph of text must explain the heading, as an extra confirmation. Because the outliner lets a writer look at the item in its menu (without any following text), then with the attached text, the writer can consider it both ways, like a user. In this environment, of course, revision of the outline often means returning to one's research, reorganizing, and then rewriting to articulate the reasoning behind the evolving structure.

And in creating an ever-expanding, ever-archiving environment of electronic information, such as a corporate Web site, one needs an up-to-date site map showing what's posted, and where, and how the menu system works (Anderson et al., 1998; Price, 1998). Just to be able to move month-old documents off the front pages and into the compost heap of an electronic magazine, an editor needs a complete hierarchical list of the site's articles, with notes indicating the original date of posting; the web-master of a small site, or the gatekeeper of a portion of a large organization's Web site may need an electronic outline simply to keep track of the growing structure, without having to browse through thousands of HTML files, in hundreds of directories, on dozens of servers. To the writer, such outlines are private menus, showing each Web page as a distinct topic, and including its date, owner, filename, and path as notes; modified slightly for users, these outlines become site maps (Anderson et al., 1998). The actual material can no longer be included within the electronic file, because the outline would soon grow too large to manipulate quickly. However, because the electronic outline can be so easily changed, it acts as a way of guiding the flow of information onto the site, checking the menus at every level, as changes are made. All of the strategies mentioned can be applied to improve the usefulness of the organization, even though a Webmaster or gatekeeper has often lost control of the actual writing in the pages being organized. In a way, electronic outlining has found its true home online.

Although electronic outlining has little theory of its own compared to hypertext, which has inspired many theorists such as those discussed in Bolter (1990), Johnson-Eilola (1994), Landow(1992), and Selber (1995), electronic outlining provides invaluable assistance to the writers who actually create the structured menu systems serving the vast majority of real-world hypertexts, which are not literary, or scholarly, but organizational, serving information en masse over the Web, or delivering CD-ROM documentation for high technology products and services. Where hypertext-creation tools such as HyperCard®, SuperCard®, HyperStudio®, StorySpace® and others make it easy to create links, they do not provide much support for analyzing and revising the structure at multiple levels for meaning and effectiveness. Even Web-page creation tools such as HomePage®, FrontPage®, and PageMill® show only the names of the various pages in an overview window, but provide nothing like the electronic outliner to examine and revise the sequence and hierarchy of menus and topics.

As a tool for reprocessing structure, then, the electronic outlining software outdoes pen and paper, word processing software, hypertext editors, and Web-page software. In Chapter 4, we will see how the old model of the outline emerged from its origins in a world of paper. Our new model—of outlining, rather than "the outline"—springs from the existence of this new electronic tool.

Because its features provide a distinct view focused on restructuring, the outlining software enables and even encourages writers to pursue multiple and interacting strategies for polishing the organization, while cycling back to note-taking and research, and forward to writing, all within the same file. And just as it gives us a new way of looking at the activities involved in arrangement of books, help systems, CD-ROMs, and Web sites, this tool also makes possible collaborative work we could not do so easily before, and lets us reflect on the nature of that extended conversation. In the next chapter I argue that this software supports collaborative creation because it acts as a temporary record of agreements, a field of reconsideration, and a living example of the social construction of knowledge, as it happens.

NOTE

[1] Here is an alphabetical list of some of the products that have included or focused on electronic outlining. Some products are currently available; others persist only on the computers of people who love them. Acta Advantage (Symmetry, Mesa, AZ), BrainForest (Aportis Technologies, Portland, OR). ClarisWorks, now Apple Works (Apple Computer, Cupertino, CA), DynaText (Inso, Providence, RI), Folio (Folio, Open Market, Burlington, MA, Provo, UT). FrameMaker+SGML (Adobe, San Jose, CA), FrameWork (Ashton-Tate, defunct), Freestyle (Summa Technologies, Kentfield, CA), Frontier (UserLand, Palo Alto, CA), Grandview (Symantec, Cupertino, CA), Inspiration (Inspiration, Portland, OR), Knowledge and Mind Amplification System (KAMAS) (Compusophic Systems, Chicago, IL), MaxThink (MaxThink, Berkeley, CA), MORE (Living Videotext, then Symantec, Cupertino, CA), Outliner (Aportis Technologies, Portland, OR), Ovation (Visual Engineering, San Jose, CA), PC-Outline (Public Brand, Cambridge, MA), PowerPoint (Microsoft, Redmond, WA), Speech Writer's Workshop Speech Outlining Software (Addison-Wesley, Reading, MA), ThinkTank (Living Videotext, then Symantec, Cupertino, CA), Three-by-Five (B.C. Software, Los Angeles, CA), Word Perfect (Corel, Salinas, CA, Ottawa, Ontario, Canada), Word (Microsoft, Redmond, WA).

3

Extending the Collaborative Conversation

All writing is conversation. Even when we write alone in our offices, we are responding to our readers' unvoiced questions, rereading the notes of subject matter experts, consulting earlier writers on the same subject, rereading our own work of yesterday as if it had been put together by a stranger. As Bazerman (1994) says, "The conversational model points up the fact that writing occurs within the context of previous writing and advances the total sum of the discourse" (p. 49).

The internal conversations with our previous draft also lead us to question our own phrases, doubt our earlier solutions, recast definitions, and, sometimes, rearrange the order of our topics. Most writers think of such muttered discussions with one's self as revolving primarily around issues of understanding and expression, perhaps because we have never recognized the extent to which we add value to our documents by organizing them well, but some of our internal debates do revolve around arrangement. In our muted conversation with previous writers, we may notice their ways of organizing the material, argue with those structures, adopt and modify. And as we meet with the members of the team with whom we are generating a document, issues of organization form an important part of the conversations.

In this chapter, I will argue that outlining software encourages and enables writers to talk together about structure on the job, and in the classroom. At work, technical writers work together in ways that span the spectrum from mere compliance to full collaboration; the degree to which the writers really work together depends on many factors, such as management commitment, personal taste, and organizational culture, but if those are favorable, then people depend on sociable routines, such as regular face-to-face meetings, and convivial tools, such as outlining software. In collaborative conversations using the outlining software as a tool, structure becomes the most valuable topic of discussion, and the most useful result. In the classroom, the teacher acts as a guide, catalyst, and coach, but the whole class pursues meaningful structure together, using the outlining software and a wall projection of the developing outline. Because it is a classroom, though, the teacher can also step in at times to point out that the activity is itself an example, a demonstration, a proof of the social construction of knowledge. So, although the work experience produces far more pages of results, the classroom provides an opportunity for reflection on the collaborative activity itself.

USING THE ELECTRONIC OUTLINER TO FURTHER CONVERSATIONS AT WORK

The technical writer must often have extensive conversations with other writers who are working on related chapters, documents, or systems, as well as with the other people on the project team—subject matter experts, managers, marketing geniuses, engineers, testers, and even some members of the target audience. In all these work situations, we commonly see a range of ways of working together on communication (Allen et al., 1987; Ede & Lunsford, 1990; Gere, 1987; Price, 1992). Here are a few points I see on that spectrum:

- *Compliance*: When a writing team is ordered to comply with standards, they often find hundreds of occasions on which they can ignore the very rules, styleguides, and editorial advisories they have been told to follow. Individuals disregard the official style; talk to the wrong audience; rearrange sections arbitrarily, all the while pretending not to notice that they are not really complying fully. Compliance, then, is a dance of apparent obedience alternating with "misunderstandings," oversights, and willful disregard. The result, for the reader, is a bumpy, disorganized, and erratic set of documents.
- *Compromise*: When disagreement surfaces on the team, each side gives up part of what they sought, in order to get their own way in another area. The result, for the reader, is often a document that is self-contradictory.

- *Cooperation*: The team may work together to produce standards, but each writer owns his or her own section, retains a personal style, and reserves the right to override group decisions during writing. Users of the document may discover it is stitched together, with confusing differences in the formatting, organization, and style of the different sections. Cooperating leaves us independent. For instance, you write one chapter, and I edit it lightly; then I write a different chapter, and you edit it lightly. We keep our distance; you're in charge of your chapter, and I'm in charge of mine. We negotiate changes, we suggest things as delicately as we can, and then live with whatever the other does. We do not really merge out best thoughts in every part. As a result, the reader encounters documents that are uneven, patchy, not thoroughly integrated. Most so-called collaboration in industry is really more in the nature of cooperation. Similarly, most computer-supported collaborative work software aids cooperation—improving electronic mail connections, joint scheduling, and mutual editing, while leaving each person the opportunity to make an individual contribution. As Duin (1991) points out, many team writers have to work asynchronously:

  > ...one person had to finish something, send it to someone else, and wait for the other person to respond on a system that often allowed text-only communication. Thus, the technology has not provided to collaborators anything close to the degree of interchange, stimulation, and speed accomplished by people working together in the same room. (p. 100)

- *Full collaboration:* As I have experienced it, this means working together so thoroughly that none of the writers end up owning any one part, chapter, or sentence. The best collaboration, I argue from my own experience, occurs when you work together in person. You have to see the other people, sense what they are thinking, picking up nonverbal cues, and responding immediately in order to move forward together. Such speed and efficiency depend on direct human contact. All intervening media, even the ones with the highest bandwidth, slow down and impede the interaction, because they filter out some of what we can perceive in less than a second, when together. Real time, in this case, is the speed at which two human beings can interact in person. Everything else is time-delayed, media-buffered, limited.

Full collaboration, as I define it here, is psychologically challenging. Collaborators must agree to argue until they reach real agreement, not a halfway compromise or acquiescence, because those so often lead to the disagreement resurfacing when the individuals write different sections, each in their own special way. Each person must speak up the moment disagreement is sensed and as long as two people disagree, the discussion must go on, no matter how long it takes—no easy voting or hand-waving to make it go away. There can be no secret reservations, to be brought up later in a fit of pique, or in elaborate foot-dragging. Everything is improvised, too, so each writer has to plunge in saying the almost-right thing, before having fully articulated it, counting on the other person to continue the idea. Each must pick up the thread of an idea when the other person loses it. First one person commands the keyboard, then the other; one leads, the other follows. The aim is to understand the material together, and produce a document that truly serves the audiences, and if any other aims creep in (such as finishing by five, or just handing something in to be done with it), the collaboration quickly dissolves. The emerging document must be mutually owned, too. Full collaborators must be willing to be paid or evaluated on the collective results. Unfortunately, good will is essential—toward each other and toward the ultimate audiences. Hard to define, easy to recognize, such a spirit goes beyond camaraderie, forcing each collaborator to confront the American cultural bias toward individualism. Individualism, in a team of writers, leads to problems for the reader, such as missing sections, predicted sections that do not appear, contradictions between sections. However, if the collaborators can reach full agreement on an outline, then, in my experience, they can go off to write the pages separately, and when those pages are brought together, they will fit like the joints of a cabinet (Price, 1992).

Routines and Tools

Writers can lay the foundation for collaboration with sociable routines and convivial tools. The team members must agree to meet regularly, for fairly long blocks of time. (The team cannot work well together if one member repeatedly skips meetings, or another shows up late, and leaves early.) The team members need to agree on housekeeping details, such as consistent file names, version control, templates, styleguides—all the mechanisms that keep a team from losing a draft in a black hole. But the key is regular face-to-face meetings, with full debriefings, so no one squirrels information away in secret or hides a problem. Unlike a conventional team meeting, in which everyone reports progress, collaborative meetings must take a problem-solving approach, to take up issues and resolve them within the meeting, rather than delegating, postponing, or voting to ignore. However, unlike traditional meetings, the collaborative meeting must also focus on creating a shared document. Matson (1996) argues that conventional business meetings have to "Convert from 'meeting' to 'doing'—where the 'doing' focuses on the creation of shared documents that lead to action. The fact is, at most computer-enabled meetings, the most powerful role for the technology is also the simplest: recording comments, outlining ideas, generating written proposals, projecting them for the entire group to see, printing them so people leave with real-time minutes. Forget groupware; just get yourself a good outlining program and an oversized monitor" (p. 123).

The best collaboration, I believe, involves direct observation of the other people, listening to what is said, challenging it immediately if one disagrees, arguing to a real conclusion, and observing, as well, all the nonverbal cues to monitor the ongoing emotional and social agreements. Writers develop such routines to make it easy (and efficient as a business activity) to work side by side.

As suggested by Illych (1973), a convivial tool is one that lets you use it to add meaning and design to your work, whereas an unconvivial tool is one that forces you to follow its quirks, bend to its will, and submit to its conventions, no matter what, if you are to succeed at wheedling out even a small transaction, such as booking an airline ticket. Zuboff (1988) and Landauer (1995), for instance, document plenty of "unconvivial" computer applications. Some electronic tools make it easier to work together, but do not guarantee conviviality. Groupware products help disseminate information quickly among team members, routing and filtering the flow, handling version control, monitoring review assignments, and generally driving the document toward publication. Other products provide various environments for conferencing among people who are not physically meeting together. Winograd and Flores (1986), inventors of a product to manage the electronic conversations within an office (the Coordinator™ Workgroup Productivity System) make a major theoretical statement when they argue "Computers are a tool for conducting the network of conversations," but then, perhaps in order to create a salable product, they focus on "conversations for action" (p. 159), and attempt to limit interoffice E-mail to exchanges in which users must explicitly identify each email as either a request or a promise, an offer or an acceptance, a report or an acknowledgement. In effect, the software forces users to adapt to its discipline, rather than changing to match the actual conversations, including, for instance, those inefficient, emotional, and rambling exchanges in which employees struggle to reach agreement on a definition, structure, or sequence of ideas—or those imaginative exchanges in which employees attempt to avoid taking any action whatsoever. Helpful as they may be, from a manager's perspective, such products encourage people to stay apart, cooperating, but not fully collaborating. However, in my experience some tools do encourage the conviviality of full collaboration: large screens, so everyone in the group can see the ongoing development of the outline (so different from scribbled notes in the margin of review copies); project management software (so all deadlines are clearly known to everyone); scheduling software (so everyone can get together), electronic mail; and, most important, electronic outlining software, as a way to record and advance the conversation in person.

Just as word processing software helps writers exchange drafts, criticize and discuss their works together, and even collaborate on documents (Costanzo, 1994; Daiute, 1986; Duin & Hansen, 1994; Ede & Lunsford, 1990; Eldred, 1989; Hawisher, 1987, 1994; Humphrey, 1987; Rodrigues & Rodrigues, 1986), electronic outlining helps a few writers work together sharing the same keyboard, looking at the same screen, as they develop a structure they can agree on. That's direct collaboration. Theorists have argued that creating hypertexts together fosters the exchange of views and consolidation of ideas in a group (Adelson & Jordan, 1992; Barrett, 1988, 1989; Barrett & Paradis, 1988; Hedden, 1992; Irish & Trigg, 1989; Johnson-Eilola, 1994), but these experiments tend to rely on software explicitly created to allow people to make hypertext links, often over networks rather than in person. Electronic outlining, because it focuses on structure more than running text or links, actually offers professional writers a better tool than either word processors or hypertext editors for collaborating where it counts, that is, at the level of organization, not links and phrases. I have seen that when a team reaches full agreement on the organization, team members can consistently carry out stylistic decisions and insert links, without having to consult each other. However, when the team has not beaten the rough edges off a structure, any attempts at individual writing go rapidly astray, resulting in patches of redundancy, inconsistency, ambiguity, failed transitions, and confusion.

An electronic outliner is an especially helpful tool for collaborating on the organization of large volumes of complex information, like that most technical writing teams face, for a number of reasons:

1. The screen displays the outline as it now stands, the keyboard lets a writer enter new material and edit, the mouse lets the writer click and reveal, or click and hide, as the team explores and reconsiders. For the first time, the evolving plan is *continuously* available in a clean, readable form, for *all* the people who are creating it. Instead of drawings on the back of envelopes, and marked-up original drafts, with blotches, the screen shows the outline as it grows, so the team can revise it intelligently.

2. By displaying the outline as the team creates it, the software forces each member of the team to look at and really think about the order of topics, the writing of each topic, the meaning of the whole. The participants see it while together, debate it, and improve it together. As Kaufer and colleagues (1993) remark in another context, "Individuals need to make their ideas visible and persuasive to themselves as well as to their collaborators" (p. 37).

3. When one writer suggests a change, everyone can see how it affects its surroundings, right away. (By contrast, think of all the suggestions given at a review meeting, in which change upon change is built on air, and no one can really foresee the net effect of all these proposed revisions until the writer sits down later, and tries to apply them all).

4. When everyone realizes that nobody knows what a particular phrase means, someone can look it up right there, or the group can assign someone to track down the facts, rather than leaving it in the outline as a placeholder.

5. Whenever a team member feels uncomfortable with a phrase, or a patch of topics, that person can speak up, forcing the others to reconsider. As Burnett (1993) points out, conflict is critical if collaborative decisions are to consider alternatives. Battling to agreement, the team members articulate contrasting models, and hash over the evidence. Everyone is forced to review the information itself, as well as the way it has been organized. As a result, everyone learns it very well. Also, the minor ambiguities that one person could tolerate will probably offend someone else, so many fuzzy patches get cleared up. The result for the reader: a structure that has been vetted from several points of view, and therefore an organization that has fewer spots of confusion.

6. The outline on screen serves as a focal point for intense conversation. As Winston Churchill once said, conversation is "The worst possible way to get things done, except for all the rest." (Plumb, 1990, p. 208). Conversation, pleasant in itself, moves the outline along, even if the outline is never complete, but always open to new input. Here is another way in which electronic text finds its way toward the new paradigm for writing envisioned by Lanham (1993)—"interactive online conversation." (p. 78). Meeting in person, but using this electronic display, the team learns from each other and comes to a series of agreements, so that any further individual work has a much greater chance of being in sync with that of everyone else than would have been the case if everyone had worked alone, and emailed sections back and forth.

The Structuring Conversation

During face-to-face conversations the team engages in many of the structural activities I described in Chapter 2, and those often lead to additional research, notes, and drafts of actual passages. In creating an online help facility for an order entry system, for instance, my partners and I started out by postulating the following sections, among others:

> Creating an Order
> Saving an Order
> Sending an Order
> Printing an Order
> Checking on an Order's Progress
> Canceling an Order
> Archiving Orders That Have Been Received

Given what we had heard from the client, this organization seemed fine, and we began to explore the next level. Creating an order seemed fairly straightforward: the user chose New from the File menu, picked a type of order (for finished goods, spare parts, or service), then filled out a two-part form (a message area, and an order area).

Unfortunately, as we got down to the level of steps, we discovered that the three different order types had wildly different forms. We were writing branches and if statements left and right ("If ordering spare parts, skip to Step 8.") We could see that the procedure was getting entirely too messy, and we wondered why the interface itself was so inconsistent. When we went back to the engineers to ask if they could consolidate the forms, or at least make them resemble each other a little more, the engineers agreed to make all the common fields look the same, so the address block, for example, would always appear in the same location, font, and layout, but they insisted that they must have three distinct forms. During this discussion, a junior engineer mentioned rather casually, "Oh, you know, the service guy never orders finished goods, and the sales people who order the finished goods don't have anything to do with service or spare parts, and usually only the boss of the service section gets to order spare parts." Suddenly we had a new perspective on the situation, one that forced us to alter our earlier high-level approach.

Now we were faced with three different users, each of whom dealt with only one kind of order. The sales people would not want to hear about spare parts and service; in fact, any mention of these topics could be confusing to the sales people. So we concluded that we should put all three order types at the top level of our structure, so users could pick their own order type, and never bother with the others. So our top two levels for these topics looked like this:

Placing a Finished Goods Order
    Creating a Finished Goods Order
    Saving a Finished Goods Order
    Sending a Finished Goods Order
    Printing a Finished Goods Order
    Checking on a Finished Goods Order's Progress
    Canceling a Finished Goods Order
    Archiving Finished Goods Orders That Have Been Received

Placing a Spare Parts Order
    Creating a Spare Parts Order
    Saving a Spare Parts Order
    Sending a Spare Parts Order
    Printing a Spare Parts Order
    Checking on a Spare Parts Order's Progress
    Canceling a Spare Parts Order
    Archiving Spare Parts Orders That Have Been Received

Placing an Order for Service
    Creating a Service Order
    Saving a Service Order
    Sending a Service Order
    Printing a Service Order
    Checking on a Service Order's Progress
    Canceling a Service Order
    Archiving Service Orders That Have Been Received

Then, as we wrote the actual procedures following the stage where the user filled out the form, we discovered that, for all three types of orders, the procedure steps were exactly the same. So we revised the organization one more time to reveal that fact, and raise more choices to the top level:

Creating a Finished Goods Order
Creating a Spare Parts Order
Creating a Service Order
Saving an Order
Sending an Order
Printing an Order
Checking on an Order's Progress
Canceling an Order
Archiving Orders That Have Been Received

A side benefit of this new organization was that each top-level menu item led directly to a step-by-step procedure, rather than a submenu, speeding up user's access to the information they might need.

The solution is a local one. In other circumstances, a different structure would be appropriate, but what is apparent, even from such a brief narrative, is that discoveries made at the lowest level sometimes have an impact at the highest level, and that research into the users' situation can, in such an open environment, lead to a restructuring to map the topics more closely to their way of thinking. Constant tinkering (clicking toward improvement) characterizes the collaborative work on structure, compared to the way most writers deal with a traditional table of contents in a document design, which is to leave it alone after the initial approval, any changes being made impromptu, without considering the overall effect.

Thus, the outlining software lets writers and other members of the team work closely together, creating and interrogating a structure down to any level, viewing it as a user might, ironing out the ambiguities, overlaps, duplications, and detours along the way. The process is fun, and gets the work done. As DeKoven (1998b) says, advocating the use of outliners in business meetings, "Key to the fun is what is actually getting done—by each person, and by all of us together. The sharing of work. The contribution of the individual magnified and multiplied by the contributions of the community" (n.p.) and the electronic outline acts as a way of recording and making visible the team's evolving agreement.

USING THE ELECTRONIC OUTLINER IN A CLASSROOM

When I teach professional writers in workshops, I often bring outlining software with me, to record and project our opinions on the wall and to help us work together to compare and choose among many alternate structures for their information systems. And when I teach undergraduates in technical writing, I sometimes use the software to encourage students to brainstorm, outline, do more research, outline, rewrite, outline, and finally to consider the emerging outline as an outward and visible manifestation of the ongoing conversation (Price, 1997d). In this section, I'll explain how I use the software in the classroom.

Preparations

As homework before class, I often ask students to read through research materials such as a set of functional specifications, a rough draft of a manual, or an earlier version of a manual we are going to revise.

In the classroom I connect a computer to equipment that displays the screen activity on the wall. In this way, I can modify whatever text we are working on, and students see the results as I type. Depending on the layout of the room, the projected image can be read by 10 to 60 students. Where possible, the computer is also networked to a printer, so I can print out the results of our class discussion and give copies to students during class.

I make it clear to students that their own individual work will grow out of the collective outline we are about to create. Individuals may have to take a section and turn that into actual procedures or reference materials. So each student has an additional, individual incentive for making sure that personal views are reflected in the emerging document, and each recognizes the need to understand how topics have been carved up and portioned out.

Brainstorming: Collaborative Invention
Using the Outliner on the Screen

With the objective of discovering all the topics we might write about, we start brainstorming. We generally follow the rule that we must accept each idea without criticizing, and students quickly get into the rhythm, suggesting their own ideas, borrowing phrases from the paper materials, sometimes explaining their contribution, sometimes just shouting it out.

To avoid burdening students with the chore of learning a new piece of software (often a real problem in computer-supported collaborative work, in my experience, and as reported by Forman, 1991), I am usually the one at the keyboard, and I type as fast as I can, to make sure I get every word right. When students have taken over the keyboard, they have complained that the pressure of typing makes it hard for them to participate in the discussion. So, although I am in control of the computer, I am acting as a servant of the discussion, and I facilitate their discussion by acting as their recording secretary. I hate blackboard brainstorming, where the facilitator listens to you talk for five minutes, then puts up one word. If someone has a 10-word heading, I take it all down. I have to practice listening, a skill not always associated with teaching, as Coles (1991) points out. If I haven't heard it all, or if I forget part, I make sure the student goes over every word, so nothing is left out.

My approach, then, resembles that advocated by DeKoven (1998a), founder of the Institute for Better Meetings, who sometimes describes this role as "technographer." He argues for using outlining software: "You take down exactly what the author tells you to take down. And you take your time, and everybody else's, to get it right" (n.p.). He distinguishes this method of recording ideas from blackboards, white boards, and flipcharts, on which people are competing for space, and the recorder therefore "interprets" or "condenses" what was said. "Using a computer, sharing a desktop, we never run out of room. There are no physical limits to how many ideas we can represent and play with at the same time. Therefore, we can allow no one the right or responsibility for interpreting our words. We can work together here. We can make things. But we must each individually contribute, and individuality takes responsibility for our contributions, because we can, and we want to, and if anybody else does, the connection gets lost: the connection between the speaker and the screen, between the speaker and the community, between the community and the work" (n.p.)

In another article, DeKoven (1995) describes this role as the Shareperson:

> Through the art of the Shareperson, everybody gets heard, recorded, represented equally....The art of the Shareperson is to make sure that we can all work on, be represented by, have access to, approval over, be empowered by the shared desktop....The Shareperson works to everyone's benefit, like a host of a barn raising. (n.p.)

As soon as someone has suggested a topic, it appears on the wall. Consider the effect. The software publishes the idea, grants it a place of honor, and places the idea at the center of discussion. Trainers say that feedback delayed is no feedback at all (Mager, 1988), so, in effect, this approach rewards each student promptly for contributions.

Occasionally one student will revise a phrase someone else has just suggested, and in this case I type both phrases. We may go on, or if a dispute breaks out, we may thrash out a resolution, rewriting one or both of the suggested topics. I point out that collaboration does not mean smiley-face acquiescence, but rather confronting real disagreement, postponing consensus, and figuring out what we really think (Burnett, 1993). Sometimes the resolution depends on going back to the original sources and rereading to come to a better understanding of the subject. In this way, even though we are officially just inventing, we are also revisiting research and reconsidering our ideas.

As the discussion continues, new ideas keep appearing, and eventually each student's contribution scrolls up out of sight. Occasionally, when inspiration stalls, I scroll back through the list. At this point, the individual's contribution has become a part of the group's product. Even if a student still feels ownership of a golden phrase, he or she can see that it has become part of a document created jointly by the class.

I leave my own ideas out, so the list belongs to the students. Authority, at first problematic in many group writing situations (Cooper &

Selfe,1990; Kremers, 1990; Moran, 1990), becomes less of a distraction when I act as their secretary; I retain authority while giving some of it away—as opposed to pretending that we are all sharing authority, as described in Zuboff (1988) and Loehr (1995). If the discussion goes well, I stay out of it; if the students get bogged down, I may ask a leading question or suggest they turn back to the paper materials for ideas. I resist adding any of my own phrases to the list, even if I know they have forgotten something important, because I have found that the subsequent work of revising the outline will usually force an encounter with missing topics. We hand the mantle of authority around, putting one person in charge, then another, reducing my grand persona as professor, and elevating their individual importance, one at a time, while granting the group as a whole the right to make major decisions. In this sense, I sometimes manage to become what Rymer (1993) describes as an instructor who is also a collaborator.

When the list reaches stasis, or everyone is exhausted, I print it out for everyone to look over. Then we focus on re-organizing the list to satisfy the needs of the various target audiences.

Coaching the Team in Outlining

Once we have the rough list of topics, I move from the role of facilitator to coach. I encourage, cheer, criticize, make suggestions, but leave the evolving document to the students. The situation is artificial because they are not my employees, or co-workers, or professional writers. In many cases what they write will not actually be used. The artificiality of a class exercise, like that of sports or games, gives us a certain freedom from consequences, but for some students, that unreality also induces a lack of seriousness, a detachment, and casual insincerity. By turning the work back over to them, I am acting as I do with professional writers in a real corporation or lab. In that sense, I am just a coach, so more of the responsibility for doing a good job falls on their shoulders.

As coach, I urge students to begin by deleting duplicates and merging topics. Performing these activities takes us through the list of topics again and again. As we get entangled in research and discussion, we gradually create a many-leveled organization and polish the language. The visual nature of the outline helps us analyze and develop quite complex structures, contrary to what Tuman (1992) feared when he imagined that in situations without a printed text, people would have no opportunity to shape "disparate thoughts into a unified document" (p. 4). On the contrary, the projected outline makes each person's idea visible, for self reflection and group study. In my class comments, I try to move all these activities out of the area of the "dimly perceived" to the explicitly recognized (Bazerman, 1994, p. 11). I point out what we are doing in each pass, naming each outlining activity—identifying additional topics, annotating a topic, deleting or merging, dividing a topic into subtopics, assembling a new topic out of others, disassembling a set of subtopics, promoting or demoting a topic, grouping, sequencing, rewriting to aid comparison, rewriting to reveal structure, and just plain writing the text under a heading. In this way, I am shifting the focus momentarily from the outline as artifact to the kind of thinking we are doing together.

As a constructivist tool, then, the software allows students to carry out the same activity on many portions of the material, learning to apply that line of thinking in many different contexts. The many activities encouraged by this software help to model another aspect of outlining—the fact that to do outlining well one must sometimes go back to research to learn more, then, on returning to the outline, one must often do some rewriting to reflect what one has learned. All three kinds of activity take place in the same electronic site.

When students recognize that we have been iteratively cycling through a number of activities that students originally thought of as occurring only in distinct stages, I see many students begin to get over their tendency to typecast the outline as a boring, arbitrary document that is supposed to be created after research and before any writing, essentially a set of notes to prove to the teacher that they have done their reading.

The recursive nature of outlining becomes clear, just as word processing helped demonstrate the looping-back dynamic process of writing (Emig, 1971; Flower & Hayes, 1981a, 1981b, 1984; Flower et al., 1990; Hawisher, 1994; Hult & Harris, 1987; Moberg, 1986; Schwarz, 1985). Students begin to see that they can go beyond the model many of them learned in high school, a variation on the distinct stages in the textbooks of Warriner, Mersand, & Griffith (1958, pp. 379-380). (First you research, then you outline, then you write). "I thought I was crazy the way I did a little of this, then a little of that," one student remarked. "But now I see that's normal."

I sometimes anthropomorphize the emerging outline as a robotic participant in our conversation, a speaker who has a better memory than the rest of us, being able to replay our latest agreement, and remind us of what we all thought a few minutes ago. "Revising this way," one student commented, "is like looking at our work as if someone else had done it." Like the extensive revisers of drafts who adopt a certain distancing to get a better picture of the text (Beach, 1976), the students get to re-see the text. Such decentering (Fitschen, 1986) makes the outline into the trace that Witte (1992) describes when he says that any meaning emerging from a document is the result of "Processes of negotiating the intellectual and emotional space between the 'self' and the 'other,' between the individual and the social, as the multiple voices of distinct constructive semi-oses mix on what might be called the battlefield of the 'trace'" (p. 287). So electronic outlining does more than allow students to carry out activities that were difficult to do over and over on paper; it provides visual evidence that we think in these ways.

Reflecting on our Social Construction

As a class we are engaged in purposeful conversation. We have an aim, but we are also talking with each other, in person. Despite our goal, we make jokes, detour off target to gossip, come back on track. The somewhat erratic path keeps the talk lively, gradually drawing people together, encouraging the shy to jump in, reverting to chat at times, then getting back to business.

As the discussion continues, I sometimes ask students to talk about what they see happening. Their comments stress several themes—their growing knowledge of the subject matter, the fact that the outline is "only temporary," and the fact that no one person owns any particular piece of the outline anymore. The outline, then, has become an outward manifestation of the ongoing conversation, a temporary record of the collective understanding to date, and a tool for thinking together.

Growing "Knowledge"

Students say that this focused set of activities forces them to come to grips with the subject matter in a detailed way many have never experienced before. "It's like really tearing it apart, and putting it back together again," said one student, whose expression suggested that he saw the assembly and disassembly of the outline as corresponding to an imaginary dissection and rebuilding of the subject matter itself. Indeed, each new outlining activity demands that the class reconsider, compare, reread, and look at component subtopics, parallel topics, and the enfolding super-topic.

The process of examining and revising the outline allows us to hear how others interpreted the phrases we thought were perfectly understandable and accurate—part of the social construction of shared knowledge, described from different perspectives by Barrett (1988, 1989), Barrett and Paradis (1989), and Bruffee (1983, 1984, 1986). Considering the subject from these perspectives, constantly revising our conception to accommodate the others, we emerge with a much more detailed understanding of the subject matter than we had at the start. "I never had to dig into something like this," one student remarked. Another commented,

"This structural approach helps me understand a lot more than what I did before, which was, well, sort of soaking stuff up by osmosis."

Students also became much more articulate. One student said with amazement, "Once you understand it, it's easy to write about." Every mature writer urges beginners to "write about what you know," but few say how a beginner can come to know something. Our collaborative outlining offers beginners one way to interrogate the subject thoroughly enough to come to "know" it, or at least, to feel comfortable with many aspects of it. They experience the way "growing understanding" can lead to facility of expression. The students were experiencing an aspect of what Kellogg (1994) refers to when he says, "Writing not only demands thinking; it is also a means of thinking." Other researchers have pointed out that writing about a subject can sharpen one's thinking about it (Bradford, 1983; Horton, 1982; Nickerson, Perkins, & Smith, 1985), as in creating legal arguments (Stratman, 1990) and scientific essays (Olsen, 1989, Olson, 1976, Olson & Atkins, 1990). In Bereiter and Scardamalia's (1987) terms, the students were going beyond simply telling what they knew to transform their knowledge through reflective thought.

Of course, there is no magical moment called *understanding*, no final conclusion we can identify as an accurate comprehension of the subject. Instead, we have our emerging interpretation of the subject, one that is very local, having been crafted for a particular audience in a particular context. That interpretation is to some degree reflected in our developing outline. I do not call this interpretation knowledge, either, because I have no certainty that we know very much; but our interpretation has become more internally coherent. It does not have as many black holes, niggling inconsistencies, and areas that make us dizzy. We are more satisfied with it as an interpretation we can present to our ultimate audience.

Students describe a change they observe in our text, too, saying that the outline has become clearer. When I probe, I find they are not thinking that we have somehow "let the subject show through," as my New Critical professors used to urge. That Platonic ideal assumed there was a real subject which could show through, refulgent, and we just had to get out of the way to let that light through. No, in the students' sense, a clear outline simply means that as writers we have considered the matter thoroughly enough to eliminate many of the verbal attributes that cause readers to scratch their collective heads—duplicate items, trivial items at the top level, key items buried out of sight, related items strewn about with no connection, a large topic treated without any attempt to divide into its components, related topics in a single list not being grouped together, topics at the same level not having any recognizable sequence, and so on. "Clear," then, is a praise word, as Robert Frost said of *poetry*, meaning that you hope the audience will regard your outline (and your document) as clear, but that is for the audience to decide. As an audience, reflecting on our own work, we feel we can see patterns quickly, recognize the reasoning behind the structures, and in repeated tests we find we can proceed without doubt, confusion, or anxiety through the structure, to reach a destination.

Recognizing that any Outline is "For Now"

Because we revise the outline in so many sessions and in so many different ways, students begin to recognize that an outline does not have to be considered a finished document, a discrete thing, but should be seen as a part of a process, and therefore always "for now." Students say they "could go on forever tinkering with this." In their binders, students may collect half a dozen printouts of the outline at various stages, each with a different time or date in the header; the paper copies are simply a way of preserving our interpretation as it was when we reached one or another convenient breakpoint and sent the text to the printer. The outline, if they think of it as a document, remains multivoiced, open, as changeable as quicksilver (compare DeKoven, 1998b; Lanham, 1990). Dobrin (1987) points out the downside of this shifting context: "As an outline expands, the meaning of the entries, the relationships among the entries, and the appropriate symbols for the entries all change...headings become subheadings, topics get split up or eliminated, and ideas or facts that we thought were telling become defanged" (pp. 102-103). The fixed becomes fluid; the definite repeatedly loses its grip on our mind. Just as the openness of a text can be externalized (Smith, 1994, p. 280) through hypertext (Balestri, 1988; Johnson-Eilola, 1994; Joyce 1988; Landow, 1992; Landow & Delany, 1993), the temporariness of all developing materials is demonstrated by the very endlessness of our activities, the fact that they seem to go on and on, and we only slow down because the bell rings, or we begin to feel we need to move on. "I never feel as if we have finished," another student said.

Abandoning Ownership

Students see that the evolving outline grows out of the whole class, shows traces of all our discussions, and does not belong to any one person. At first, people still show pride of ownership when we turn our attention to one of their phrases, but gradually they let go and even take part in revising text they first contributed. DeKoven (1998a), observing a similar phenomenon, sees three phases—collecting, connecting, and correcting. "After individual comments are captured ("collect"), the group organizes the individually authored contributions into logical, group-authored categories ("connect"). These categories (level one) are produced by and agreed on and are the property of everyone. The individual contributions (level two) substantiate each category. The outline, collapsed to the first level, reveals the consensus, collectively authored, produced, and owned" (n.p.). I haven't found the process quite as neat as that; in fact, I would argue that at every level, the attachment to one's own words gets loosened. The words do not have signatures attached, and most students say that eventually they cannot recall who said what. In my experience, the evolving document then represents an agreement, or consensus, like that of some experiments in classroom collaborative writing (Daiute, 1986; Goldstein & Malone, 1985), but what strikes participants more strongly is their ability to give up ownership. Some students notice that they no longer even remember which phrases they contributed. This sense of surprised detachment is especially striking when they realize they are looking at something they themselves contributed earlier—without recognizing it as their own. One student laughed out loud at a good joke in one outline, and was surprised to hear that she was the one who had added it in the first place.

The idea that writing is a solitary task, and the corollary that an outline is one person's work, lies deep in our culture. In working together on this evolving outline, these students discover that they can do verbal work collaboratively, and that this document is a social construction. They begin to recognize that this process resembles what they do when they consult with a peer, late at night, discussing a paper, so they edge toward Rubin's (1988) view that all writing is collaborative because it involves conversations with other people. They do not go as far as Bakhtin in denying individual ownership to every document (Bakhtin, 1981, 1986; Bakhtin & Volosinov, 1986) but they see that "This represents all of us, and it doesn't matter how many words I got into it, or didn't get into it," as one student said. Furthermore, the whole process comes to be considered a large conversation, as Halliday (1978) suggested, "not something that has a beginning and an ending. The exchange of meanings is a continuous process" (p. 136).

In this chapter, we have seen how the evolution from pen and paper to electronic media has brought us a software tool that dramatically shifts attention from the outline as a momentary product to outlining as an ongoing process, in which structural analysis and constructive thinking are played out on the screen, as many previously half-conscious activities become visible, and the group takes advantage of the very presence and changeableness of the emerging outline to watch the collaborative writing unfold.

We have managed, at least for a few hours, to shift the focus from the document to the process, from the individual to the group, and from the primacy of the written to the sheer overwhelming presence—embedded in any written document—of the conversation itself.

This picture of what outlining can help us do seems quite different from the one many of us received in school. To clarify the distinction, I will devote the next two chapters to the old school model of the outline, which has always been implicit in textbooks, but rarely made explicit as a full theory. I am going back in time, to show how heavily the old model was influenced by the medium of paper, and how, once the model became entrenched, it was defended with arguments about logic, practicality, and growth—arguments that despite their creakiness, point to some of the real benefits of outlining.

In the final chapter of the book, I will draw on this contrast between the paper and electronic perspectives, to create a new, overarching model of the activity of outlining. I argue that the new medium, and its software, makes this theoretical model visible, and emphasizes the process aspects over the product, while encouraging us to work together and then notice how—and why—we enjoy collaborating.

II

A Look Back

4

The Paper Model

In the last two chapters, we have explored the features and capabilities of electronic outlining software. We have seen how this software enables the writer to undertake substantial and continuous restructuring of the material, using the outline as a working view of the material while taking notes, organizing the information, and writing, and we have also seen how the software helps writing teams to work more closely together, and, in some cases, to reflect on the social nature of the construction of the document, as it grows during extended and multiple conversations recorded and made visible in the expanding outline. Now we can look back at earlier conceptions that culminated in the "outline" as modeled in school textbooks of the last 50 years, and discern how heavily that model was influenced by the media it unconsciously assumed—paper and pen.

Johnson (1997) points out that our era's rapid development of new media—the "sheer velocity with which technology now advances" (p. 4)—gives us a historically unique opportunity to compare one medium after another, seeing how each affects our worldview. He says:

> We can grasp the way different media shape our habits of thought because we can see the progression, the change from one form to another. You're born into a world dominated by television, and then suddenly you find yourself acclimating to the new medium of the World Wide Web. The shift is startling, even thrilling, depending on your mindset—but however you respond to the new forms, their arrival has an illuminating force. (pp. 4-5)

Having immersed ourselves in electronic outlining, then, let us use the software as a contrasting background for a look at earlier ideas of the outline. Outlining emerges from the great tradition of rhetoric, but becomes possible only when writers are familiar with the book as a medium (printed or not), as opposed to the scroll—because on each of the book's distinct pages, the medieval copyists separated out headings, numbered individual verses, and used graphic devices to distinguish paragraphs—designing all the raw materials that would be needed, later, for an outline. Immersed in this culture of the book, both hand-made and printed, Renaissance rhetoricians recommended crude proto-outlines to students who had to prepare speeches for court, church, or diplomacy. In the 16th century Ramus strongly recommended outlining, and his success among Puritan ministers seems to have influenced early scientific writers in the 17th century. In the 18th and 19th century, the success of scientific taxonomies and classification schemes may have given another boost to the outline as a form. Extensive note-taking, like that of Charles Darwin and the makers of the first *Oxford English Dictionary*, probably also nudged writers toward the outline as a way of taming the mass of data. Finally, rhetoric teachers in the 19th and 20th century codified the outline as a school exercise. Composition and technical writing textbooks of the last 50 years summarize this school model, while advocating it with various degrees of enthusiasm. Thus, a document that probably began as a crude aid to invention and organization—like a set of notes on a whiteboard—grew into a clearly defined formal genre, a carefully carved stick with which teachers and textbook authors could beat many generations of students. This chapter, then, considers how that history, and the media used, shaped the way the outline came to be thought about, explained, and justified, in these textbooks.

The next chapter considers the ways in which these textbook authors, most of whom were proponents of outlining, argued on its behalf, despite the difficulties of using paper to carry out the activity. Ironically, the benefits that these textbook authors hoped for may turn out to be more easily achieved now that outlining has gone electronic. (In the final chapter of the book, I will endeavor to sketch out a new theory of outlining, moving beyond the school model, but recognizing its aspirations).

The Importance of the Medium

Clearly, the medium in which we regularly create communications will eventually influence our intellectual model of what we have created, and how we created it (Bolter, 1991; Heim, 1993; Innis, 1951; Johnson, 1997; Johnson-Eilola, 1994; Landow, 1992; McLuhan, 1962, 1964a, 1964b). I use the term *medium* to refer to any substance or combination of substances that people can shape, mark or manipulate into dozens of discrete units, which can then be put together into thousands of combinations, which in turn can be built into an infinite number of different communications. To carve those shapes, make those marks, or organize those units, people use one or more tools. When a society adopts some combination of media and tools for semiotic purposes, we have a communication technology. For writers, the media combination of paper and ink has come to dominate the last half-millenium as our technological icon—that is, an emblem we worship, a concrete and outward manifestation of our ideas about written communication, and also, in our imagination, a constraint, limiting our idea of what writing can be.

Just as our thinking is influenced by the actions we perform on a regular basis, those actions are enabled or constricted by the media and tools we use. We tend to think of what we are doing in terms of what we see in front of us, what we manipulate, and what products we see emerge—all of which differ from one medium to another, and, to a lesser extent, from one tool to the next. In turn, the combination of media and tools—the technology—concretizes these ideas, stands for them, helps us represent them to ourselves. In this sense, any technology can potentially act as an "object-to-think-with," to borrow Papert's phrase describing a) the differential gears he played with as a child, b) Lego™ blocks that children use for construction, and c) Logo™, the program he created to allow children to learn vector geometry by tinkering with a microworld. (Papert, 1980, p. 11; 1997, pp. 68-70; see also Barrett & Paradis, 1988, p. 157). The technology affects our activities as we write, and we learn what "writing" is by building up a set of strategies, materials, and tools we can handle and manipulate, so, in the end, that microworld or culture offers us a set of metaphors through which we think about writing. As Daiute (1985) says:

> The writing instrument itself can affect the cognitive process. The instrument can stifle the mental dynamism of writing, enhance it, or make no difference at all. As inscribed clay tablets dried, the writer in ancient times had to feel that the work was complete. In contrast, a writer who is using a computer tends to feel that the process is ongoing....The computer is the perfect tool for a *process* approach to writing, because it makes revising and recopying texts physically easy. (pp. 66-67)

The traditional idea of the outline—as presented by some 75 composition, rhetoric, and technical writing textbooks published over the last 50 years—contains many attributes derived from the medium, as we can see more clearly now that we have another medium for contrast. What we are looking at, then, is a model that developed through the actual practice of some writers, and, gradually became a standard assignment in schools, to judge by this sampling of textbooks.

The authors of these textbooks, as a group, show a strong, almost religious attachment to the medium of paper and ink, and, with a vision conditioned largely by their experience with paper documents, many of these writers continue to see notes, outlines, and drafts as discrete documents, each produced at a different stage. For most of these textbook authors, the advent of the typewriter, a new tool for an old medium, did not disturb this kind of thinking. Only in the last five years or so, with the benefit of 25 years of word processing, and a dozen years of electronic outlining, do a few textbook authors explicitly recognize that the same electronic file can contain notes, outline, and draft.

Media are not easy to find or develop; but once a new medium has become popular in a society, people create many new tools for working it, and then start "improving" those tools. Early users of a new technology (new media and new tools together) tend to see it as a way of doing exactly what an earlier technology did, only better, but once people have used the new technology intensively, they develop new activities, transform previous practices, or relegate those practices to a minor role. For instance, copying had formed the core activity in the monastic scriptoria for hundreds of years, but, after Gutenberg, the practice gradually dwindled to a minor chore on the way to print (Daiute, 1985; Tuman, 1992). When video first appeared as a medium ordinary people could use, the early adopters imitated film, the medium of choice for both cinema and broadcast television until then. However, as more people explored this medium, they discovered what it could do uniquely well, and stopped trying to make costume epics or high-resolution Kodak scenes; instead people take cameras out in the open air and into meeting rooms, making live cameras part of real-time art installations (Price, 1977).

As people get used to a new technology, then, and see new possibilities for action, they begin to change their ideas about the products they turn out, and to redefine the whole process. After a while, people are "working in" the medium. They exploit its options, chafe at its limitations, but accept them, and work around them. Soon, those constraints begin to limit the way practitioners think.

Meanwhile, many people who are accustomed to the earlier media and tools retain their loyalty to them, and view the new technologies as intruders, bringing a decline in values (Tuman, 1992, p. 41), or, if they felt claustrophobic before, a breath of fresh air. Today's students, having less experience with ink pens, tend not to romanticize them as many of their elders do.

Many of these textbook authors show great loyalty to the paper and ink they grew up with, and even authors who know and use word processing tend to talk as if the computer is just an interesting plus, if a student happens to want to do a little more than can be done with pen and paper, or typewriter and paper. The authors have not really changed their conception of a document from "a paper," to an electronic communication that can be displayed, printed, or transmitted. These authors still use ideas that were shaped by paper experiences, and downplay or ignore the benefits, challenges, and ideas that come with computing. These authors almost never forefront the question of which media and tools will work best for their students. On the whole, these authors show a benign indifference to the impact of media.

Of course, anyone's choice of media and tools is usually overdetermined. Career aims, current work situation, class, finances, supervisors, clients, customers, local organizations all drive people toward certain media, and within those media, to particularly hot tools, offered by a technologically abundant culture (Apple, 1986, p. 171; Bell, 1975, p. 168; Tuman, 1992, p. 42). In some environments, like the university, people can experiment with unfamiliar technologies, or drag their feet and refuse, but in most occupations, people have little control over the decision.

However the vast majority of these textbook authors—up to the last five years or so—act as if the technology one uses when creating an outline makes little difference. At best, some authors acknowledge that students might want to use word processing to create outlines—clearly, an add-on to the important discussion, which remains remarkably innocent of the deep influence of a medium and its tools, as if nothing significant had changed with the advent of electronic outlining.

Electronic outlining, as we have seen, speeds up the creation of an outline out of notes, encourages rather than discourages revision of the structure, and allows the writer to draft portions of the text on the fly, while glancing at the surrounding outline. The computer-enabled formatting helps identify structure automatically, relieving the writer of the painful chore of inserting labels, then revising them when a single change is made. Because any changes appear "neatly typed," writers do not get bogged down deciphering patches of squiggles and arrows. The impersonal but clean display of the text on screen and in printouts can also give the writer more objective distance from the material, in a way that one's own handwriting does not. Because the document is electronic, change becomes the norm; there is no "final product," simply a series of snapshots in the form of printouts, whenever the writer reaches a pause, or a deadline. At the same time, skimming becomes more difficult, leading users to fold up sections not being worked on, and to unfold the subtopics as necessary, leading to a sense of structure as opening and closing, hiding and revealing, or containing—rather than simply marching forward through the numbering system. The writer becomes a user, as well as creator, and sees the outline as a structure to move through, and modify, a live system. But the vast majority of these textbook authors seem to assume that students will still mainly be using paper and ink for research, outlining, drafting, and revising. And for these textbook authors, paper is always primary—paper in the form of note cards, outlines, drafts, and, of course, final versions of student "papers."

HOW OUTLINES FIRST APPEARED ON PAPER

Outlines in some form have been with us since the early days of printing, and perhaps since parchment replaced papyrus. We do not know who cobbled together the first outline—perhaps a list of topics and subtopics, with some visual indication of sequence and hierarchy—as a plan for a speech or document, but we can guess at some of the precursors and preparations.

The classical rhetoricians consistently offered their students a kind of outline as a template, when they discussed arrangement. We do not have any evidence that students of the classical rhetoricians made anything we would recognize as outlines for their speeches, but the fact that their instructors provided a list of the parts of a conventional speech (a list that varied from one instructor to another) meant that students began with what we would call a high-level outline of the oration, into which all their invention could pour. Imagine being handed this template:

- Exordium
- Narratio
- Confirmatio
- Refutatio
- Peroratio

Understanding the rhetorical purpose of each conventional section, the students were then to adjust the disposition of topics among these sections according to the type of speech, the subject, their own ethos, and their audience. Because of these considerations, the process could not be done mechanically. The students had to think whether a particular idea, story, or fact would work best in the introduction, the narration, the proof, or perhaps, the section attacking the opposition's ideas. Finally, the question arose: should this topic be brought up again in the conclusion? In *De Inventione* (*I*, sections xxi-xvii), Cicero (1949) urges the speaker to list the parts of a speech in a section he calls the *partitio*, which divides up and displays the parts of the speech to come, acting as an overview or advanced organizer of the components that will follow. He does not describe an outline as we envision one, but he does view the partition as a methodical statement of the topics to come, a blueprint that must be followed section by section, "in order one after another as they have been planned in the partition." (I, xxiiii, 33). This manner of thought, maintained throughout the Dark and Middle Ages, may have laid the foundations for structural thinking that led the Renaissance to develop the outline as a model for a speech or document.

Similarly, early versions of tables of content offered another precursor model for what we think of as an outline. For instance, in the 1st century, having written 36 books of his *Natural History*, Pliny the Elder (1944, 1998) added another book which was nothing but a list of the contents of the others, with sources, arranged book by book (a three-level hierarchy). But a table of contents simply records the major sections of a work that has already been compiled, whereas an outline, as we are concerned with it, helps the writer create a plan for a work in progress. So, although these rudimentary tables of contents may have reenforced the model of a hierarchical list as a brief representation of the structure of a longer document, they were not functioning the way we think of an outline—as a tool for development. That work was reserved for later rhetoricians.

By the 4th century, most writers in areas that did not produce papyrus—particularly Christians—had generally adopted parchment (rectangular sheets of the skin of goats, sheep, or calves) or the finer vellum (sheets made from the skins of younger animals) instead of papyrus, fitting together these pages into volumes called codexes that we would recognize as books. Greeks and Romans had long used a pair of waxed wooden tablets, tied together by metal rings or leather thongs, for on-the-spot calculations in business and construction; gradually, sheets of papyrus and later parchment were slipped in between these "covers," and over time these leaves came to be bound together, and attached to the wooden covers. Copyists and creators now took advantage of the new medium to widen the columns in which they wrote, and to write on both sides of the pages (Bolter, 1991; Innis, 1958; Microsoft, 1997; Ong, 1982).

This change in medium, though not as important culturally as the decline of the oral tradition or the later spread of printing, had a major impact on people's idea of what a document could be (Bolter, 1991; Innis, 1951, Ong, 1982). The resulting codexes were tougher, larger, safer to transport, and easier to flip through than the older, more fragile papyrus scrolls (Innis, 1951). Able to handle many sheets at a time, the codex encouraged combining numerous documents into a single volume, so that the New Testament could be presented as a single book, rather than a set of individual rolls. Over the next centuries, as papyrus supplies were cut off by the Mohammedans, and as more monasteries were founded with the preservation of books as a sacred duty, the monks worked out a

design that began with the parchment page as the basic element of layout
(rather than the roll). Text, instead of being conceived as an unending
river, was locked up in a frame. Art, no longer just the pale washes possible on papyrus, took on detail and vivid color, and had to be worked into
the same frame as the text, sometimes as decoration, sometimes as the
main event; the interaction between a specific illustration and a particular
passage of text became a challenge, making the monastic designers more
and more aware of the distinct chunks of text they were dealing with.
Over hundreds of years, headings (the title of a book, the title of a chapter) rose to prominence. Individual verses got their own decorated initial
letters, paragraphing, and numbers. In fact, the idea of a paragraph as a
graphic indicator of a distinct passage was probably born, somewhere in
the Dark Ages, as a method for visually setting off a line of verse, or a sentence or two of the Bible. Thus, the switch from papyrus to parchment,
making possible these early books, may have launched design elements
we still employ in the outline—headings, lines, individual paragraphs,
initial labels (derived from decorated initial letters), and numbered sections.

In addition to these elements, the tree diagram arose as a way of showing a genealogy or branching categories as early as Cassiodorus (died ca.
585), and continued to expand throughout the Middle Ages, a verbo-
visual diagram of a hierarchical structure (Bolter, 1991, p. 74). And as the
codex became more popular, authors of encyclopediac works developed
"more elaborate categories and deeper hierarchies" (Bolter, 1991, p. 90)
to encompass all their material in tables of contents, or frameworks we
would think of as outlines.

The advent of paper made all manner of writing cheaper, and therefore more plentiful. From its beginnings in China in the 1st century,
paper quickly became the basis for woodblock printing, but only came to
Europe in the 12th century, thanks to the Moors, taking hold in Italy in
the 13th century, and expanding into the rest of Europe during the 14th
century. With a pen, paper provided a cheap, discardable medium for
temporary information—notes, personal letters, bills of lading, invoices,
accounts. For the developing printing trade, paper provided a surface
that worked well with the equipment and inks, so that printers could issue
smaller, cheaper books to challenge the copyists, whose huge vellum volumes took so much time to make, and cost so much (Innis, 1951). The
printed paper books carried forward the design motifs invented for
parchment, mechanizing their creation, but not substantially modifying
their function. For writers, paper made all the aspects of pre-writing
more convenient—note-taking, planning, sketching out a rough draft.
Renaissance rhetoricians seem to have taken advantage of this new ability
to train students and other writers on paper, not just outloud, or on eras-

able wax tablets—media in which the creations soon disappeared, making them hard to reuse and analyze at a later time (compare Rouse & Rouse, 1989).

Because invention and arrangement had remained at the core of the rhetorical tradition from Aristotle through the Middle Ages, the idea of a fitting topics into a conventionally defined structure came easily to schoolmasters of the Renaissance. Topics could be summarized in headings, which in turn became branches in elaborate tree diagrams and similar diagrams (Bolter, 1991, pp. 16-21, 74-76; Ong, 1958, pp. 74-83, 104-130, 199-202, 314-318).

In working on arrangement, then the Renaissance rhetoricians advocated early forms of outlining in their teaching. For instance, assuming that his readers are familiar with bound volumes (whether printed or not), Erasmus (1990/1512) advises youngsters to make up a commonplace album by starting with a full list of subjects, such as the main types and subdivisions of vice and virtue, plus prominent or common events. Each topic gets its own heading, and all its subtopics become subsections under that, and under each of those subheads one can drop any interesting story, idea or *bon mot* one hears.

> So prepare for yourself a sufficient number of headings, and arrange them as you please, subdivide them into the appropriate sections, and under each section add your commonplaces and maxims; and then whatever you come across in any author, particularly if it is rather striking, you will be able to note down immediately in the proper place, be it an anecdote or a fable or an illustrative example or a strange incident or a maxim or a witty remark or a remark notable for some other quality or a proverb or a metaphor or a simile. (Assembling Illustrative Material) (p. 551)

In 1512, Erasmus argues that dropping these quotations into this hierarchy of headings fixes the commonplaces in one's memory, and helps one make use of what one reads, because "Whatever the occasion demands, you will have the materials for a speech ready to hand, as you have all the pigeonholes duly arranged so that you can extract just what you want from them" (p. 551). Hence, a prepared (but empty) outline encourages systematic note-taking, in preparation for speeches on these topics.[1]

Wilson's *Arte of Rhetorique* (1990) reflects his own school-teacherly devotion to outlining, with a proliferation of headings at three levels (one for each paragraph, section, and chapter), summary paragraphs that end in lists announcing the subtopics to be covered in the following subsections, and numbered lists introducing sections which contain these items as subsections (each again with its own numbered heading). To a modern eye, the book looks like an expanded outline. One imagines that as a tutor in the late 1540s and early 1550s, Wilson may have demanded that his noble and gentle tutees develop their speeches in this way, as preparation for future careers as English lawyers, politicians, or public servants (Schoeck, 1983). Certainly, some form of outline seems to have been used in the 16th century France by officials preparing letters and reports. As a Gentleman of the Chamber for Henri III, and Henri of Navarre, Montaigne (1580), for instance, boasts of beginning to write without any outline or plan, just writing one word after another—which he clearly conceives of as contrary to the conventions followed at court.

In the same period, Puritan ministers learned to use crude outlines to prepare sermons, following Ramus' (1543) advice in the *Dialecticae partitiones*:

> Sett forthe shortly the some of the text, which thou hast taken in hand to interprete: next...porte thy text into a fewe heads that the auditor may the better retaine thy sayings: Thirdly...intreate of every heade in his owne place with the ten places of invention...and last...make thy matter playne and manifest with familiar examples & aucthorities out of the worde of God....(quoted in Miller, 1939, p. 338)

Ramus recommended that the writer follow a routine with four stages: 1) begin with a summary, 2) write down some major ideas about it as headings, 3) expand on and explain those ideas in text, and 4) add citations and examples in the text, to make the meaning clear.

Through these stages, a minister could develop a standard organization starting with an overview, offering key interpretative ideas as headings, following each heading with a doctrinal explanation of the text, continuing with examples, more quotations, and ways to apply the doctrine to the audience's life. This organization also had a standard visual format—summary, headings that express the gist of the points so the audience can remember them, occasionally followed by subheads and then text expanding on the idea with examples and further citations (Batschelet, 1988, pp. 288, 291).

Ramus undertook to reduce all previous knowledge to a series of outlines that could be printed for the use of students; he saw these outlines as a way students could learn—and quickly memorize—his own overview of rhetoric and philosophy going back to Aristotle and Plato. As Ong (1958) says, Ramus' outlines presented "a reorganization of the whole of knowledge and indeed of the whole human lifeworld" (p. viii). Looking back to the Ramus as the progenitor and propagandist of the printed outline, Heim (1993) agrees with Ong that Ramus represents the flowering of print:

Ramus advocated knowledge outlines. The printing press could reproduce any number of pages displaying graphic trees that present summaries of a body of knowledge. Each page is a skeletal outline of a subject arranged systematically, with the branches on the tree showing how the parts of the subject matter connect. The printed page thus becomes a chart of topics divided into dichotomies with their parts and interconnections made clearly visible. That is, the printed Ramist text is a visual encyclopedia of cultural literacy in which topics and their parts appear in a nutshell." (p. 43)

Ramus converted to Protestantism in 1561, and died during the Saint Bartholomew's Day massacre of Protestants (Ong, 1958). In part because of his conversion and martyrdom, and in part because of his intellectual approach, his works won a wide audience among Protestant scholars, particularly Puritans. His dialectical outlines, dividing a topic into a series of dichotomies that branched and branched to the edge and bottom of the page persuaded several generations of scholars that this method was a rigorous way to analyze almost any topic.

Science seems to have followed the rhetorical lead of religion. For instance, in discussing the way early American scientific writing grew out of the Puritan sermon, Batschelet (1988) shows how Samuel Danforth's 17th century book on Halley's comet includes a series of minor headings under the major headings, in a way we would recognize as similar to an outline. For instance, Danforth (1665) starts with the major heading, "1. The Comet is no sublunary meteor or sulphureous exhalation, but a Celestial Luminary, moving in the starry Heavens" (p. 291). Batschelet shows how Danforth relates subheads to that major heading:

The heads are sometimes supported by proofs, statements of subordinate facts; for example, to support head 1 given above, Danforth supplies the following proofs,

The Truth therefor may be demonstrated.
1. By the vast Dimensions of it's (sic) body...
2. By the smallness of it's Parallax....
3. By it's large circular motion...
4. By it's long duration and continuance...
5. By it's Visibility to all Countries and Nations...

At other points the heads are supported by data such as dates, longitudes, and latitudes. (Batschelet, 1988, p. 291)

Officials, ministers, and scientists of the 16th and 17th century, then, may have begun planning their writing by setting down key headings and subheads, and even numbering the subheads, in what we would call a rough outline.

In the 18th century we begin to see writers, rhetoricians, and philosophers using the term "outline" to refer to a quick but incomplete glimpse of what is to come, or, as the 1933 edition of the *Oxford English Dictionary* says, "a description, giving a general idea of the whole, but leaving details to be filled in." The citations indicate an emphasis on the very sketchiness of the outline, as if it were a painter's preliminary drawing. For instance, the dictionary cites Steele in 1710, saying in *Tatler* No. 182, "His Drama at present has only the Out-Lines drawn."(p. 6). In 1718, Murray, in the introduction to his *English Grammar*, proposes to offer "A distinct general view, or outline, of all the essential parts of the study"(p.8). In 1751, Hume in his *Essays and Treatises*, talks of "The faint rudiments, at least, or out-lines, of a general distinction between actions." (Part II, p. 249). We may hear the influence of artists' practice here, drawing charcoal sketches to rough out the large elements of a composition, without getting too precise; at the same time, the writers may be increasingly aware of the visual nature of an outline, even when constructed of text. The term *outline*, then, seems to bring overtones from the visual arts, to describe a verbal practice.

In 1828 the rhetorician Whately (1990) stresses the graphic and psychological benefits of an outline because it offers a brief visual preview of the contents of a composition—providing a striking miniature of the proposed larger composition, easy to remember, but loose enough to be overridden during drafting. He argues that teachers ought to require many such outlines from their students—as long as the teachers "sedulously" correct them, pointing out applicable general rules. Whately phrases this advice in a way that suggests he may be reflecting (and correcting) many years of pedagogical practice:

Drawing up of outlines or skeletons
It should be added, as a practical rule for all cases, whether it be an exercise that is written for practice's sake, or a composition on some real occasion, that an outline should be first drawn out, — a skeleton as it is sometimes called,—of the substance of what is to be said. The more briefly this is done, so that it does but exhibit clearly the several heads of the composition, the better: because it is important that the whole of it be placed before the eye and the mind in a small compass, and be taken in as it were at a glance; and it should be written therefore not in sentences, but like a table of contents. Such an outline should not be allowed to fetter the writer, if, in the course of the actual composition, he find any reason for deviating from his original plan. It should serve merely as a track to mark out a path for him, not as a groove to confine him. But the practice of drawing out such a skeleton will give a coherence to the Composition, a due proportion of its several parts, and a clear and easy arrangement of them; such as can rarely be attained if one begins by completing one portion before thinking of the rest. And it

will be found a most useful exercise for a beginner, to practise—if possible under the eye of a judicious lecturer—the drawing out of a great number of such skeletons, more than he subsequently fills up; and likewise to practice the analysing in the same way, the Compositions of another, whether read or heard. (p. 842)

Interestingly, in 1877, in his *Science of Rhetoric* (1990), the American Hill attempts to systematize rhetoric as a method of "producing mental changes" (p. 881) in the audience. He discards traditional notions of arrangement, but his very emphasis on system leads him to provide a detailed three-level outline of his entire book, as a table accompanying this panegyric for his "scientific" approach (p. 880). His defense sounds like Ramus:"A systematic analysis, by insuring a progressive exposition and avoiding repetition, enables the learner to master the whole work in a very short time" (p. 879).

Indeed, as science moved toward classifying the natural world during the 18th and 19th centuries, the layout of heads and indented subheads in an outline seems to have been given new cachet. Scientific taxonomies and other categorization schemes gave dramatic evidence of the usefulness of numbered, bulleted, and indented outlines. Following the developing conventions of the field of biology, for instance, Charles Darwin started a new project by sorting his information spatially. He relied on portfolios of notes, open shelves for sorting books and papers, multiple complex cabinets with wide labeled drawers (Darnton, 1996, p. 4) , books with personal indexes he made up in the back, and paper indexes on separate sheets for books he had had to return to other people. To draw all this material together, he relied on outlining:

> With my large books I spend a good deal of time over the general arrangement of the matter. I first make the rudest outline in two or three pages, and then a larger one in several pages, a few words or one word standing for a whole discussion or series of facts. Each one of these headings is again enlarged and often transferred before I begin to write *in extenso*. As in several of my books facts observed by others have been very extensively used, and as I have always had several quite distinct subjects in hand at the same time, I may mention that I keep from thirty to forty large portfolios, in cabinets with labeled shelves, into which I can at once put a detached reference or memorandum. I have bought many books, and at their ends I make an index of all the facts that concern my work; or, if the book is not my own, write out a separate abstract, and of such abstracts I have a large drawer full. Before beginning on any subject I look to all the short indexes and make a general and classified index, and by taking the one or more proper portfolios I have all the information collected during my life ready for use. (Darwin, 1889, pp. 79-80)

By the beginning of the 20th century the outline appears in media we find familiar: ink or pencil on standard-sized sheets of paper, often with ruled lines to write on. Given the media, the writer can indicate structure by arranging individual headings (and whole paragraphs) using indentation, depth, and prefixed numbers and letters, following some convention or other. The main visual tools in the paper outline are white space, starting horizontal position (how far from the left margin?), vertical position in relation to the next higher topic (how far down?), and labels at the beginning of each topic. Each chunk is conceived of as a distinct topic, in its own paragraph, whether it is a single phrase, a sentence, or a heading with subordinate material attached. Thus, paper and ink provide several ways to distinguish between units in a complex hierarchy—and, because the paper outline itself is distinct from any notecards one may have developed, this medium suggested to many people that essentially an outline must be a different physical object, distinct from the notecards, related only intellectually.

HOW NOTES APPEARED ON CARDS

For more than 50 years, textbook writers have recommended that their students record their research on note cards, a medium that seems to have developed as an improvement on cut or torn slips of paper such as those originally used for citations in the *Oxford English Dictionary*. Clear (1993) describes the context for those citation slips:

> During the nineteenth century in Britain, the scientific community working in the area of philology and related disciplines became increasingly concerned with data gathering as a proper preliminary to serious scientific investigation. Compilation of the *Oxford English Dictionary* (OED), a monumental work of scholarship in lexicography, was based from the beginnings in the 1860s on the painstaking collection of citations from text. (p. 164)

In the 1870s and 1880s, when James Murray was recruiting volunteers to send in citation slips for terms that would end up defined in the *Oxford English Dictionary*, he was paying his children a penny an hour to collate these scraps of paper (Willinsky, 1994, p. 38). How grateful I imagine those children would have been to receive the quotations on what we now call index cards—they may be bulkier, but they're so much easier to sort, stack, group, and divide!

During the same period, as more and more professionals published books that others in their discipline had to read, and as more people became readers, the growing number of public libraries had to list their books not in order of acquisition, or by room, but by author, title, and subject, for easier lookup. Dewey's decimal system (launched in 1876) and the emerging card catalogs popularized a move from bound notebooks and paper to sets of interchangeable cards (Jackson, 1974).

The invention and commercial distribution of cheap cards one could write on, often with an open space at the top for headings and light blue lines for script, helped any scholar study a single document while taking individual notes on many different topics. After having read dozens or even hundreds of books, the scholar could sort the notes by category rather than source, drawing out his or her own themes, grouping a number of quotations in order to come up with a personal synthesis. By the 1940s, these cards were so easily available even students could afford them, and textbook authors felt no hesitation sending their readers out to the stationery store for a supply.

As a medium, then, these cards helped anyone trying to organize a collection of notes. At creation, each note became a separate chunk of information, not a sentence or two buried in a page, or a paragraph hidden somewhere in a multi-page document. The note card held the chunk of information as an individual object, so now a researcher could sort those objects, group them, divide them into subcategories, and sequence them in many different arrangements, just by flipping cards. The scholar was not held back by the recalcitrant sheaf of paper, containing multiple information objects on each page.

In practice, note cards provide a way to organize complex material by laying out piles of topics on a broad surface. The student can arrange the piles in a certain order. The layout of the piles tends to burn itself into the mind, as a person sorts the cards. As the student makes a decision about each card, the mind is, in effect, reconsidering the overall structure of the material. By engaging the sensations of movement, appealing to the eye, and demoting for the moment the detailed text, focusing instead on the headings alone, notecards provide a kinesthetic, visual, and verbal impression of the intellectual organization.

In this way, the medium encourages constant reorganization. Santmyers (1949) says:

> You are urged to adopt, without hesitation, a loose-card method for planning and outlining reports....With only one topic to a card you can shift the order of the cards in any manner you see fit. By merely moving a card, you can see how a topic will look here or look there in your plan. If you cannot find a suitable and fitting place for it, you can put it aside for the time being and go ahead with the arrangement of your other topics. As you pick up each card, you can examine the topic on it objectively—look it as it is, a thing in itself. (p. 32)

Freed from the role of sentence or paragraph in an unending stream of text on a long sheet of paper, the note takes on its own life, as an independent object, one that can be placed in some new relationship to other objects. Santmyers (1949) stresses the analogy with an engineer putting together a model.

> The principle involved is as old as planning itself. When planning, free the mind for the hard work of thinking—for thinking about the things that cannot be seen; put the things that can be seen into such shape or form that they can be looked at by themselves, can be moved easily and quickly, to be tried in different combinations, or can be completely discarded. The engineer and mechanics are following this principle when they build a model or make a template. (pp. 32-33)

Smith (1940) foresaw the need for regularly reshuffling the organization, dealing out the cards in new combinations as one learns more about the subject.

> This allows you to rearrange and regroup your cards at stated intervals as your work proceeds. Such elasticity of organization is necessary, for you will find that often your subject will take a new direction, or an altered emphasis while being investigated. (p. 272)

Some textbook authors who favor the note card seem to do so because they recognize that the writer will need to reorganize the material regularly during research, to figure out what else to look up (Sypherd et al., 1957, p. 143), to ensure that no key material gets left out (USGS, 1957, p. 9), and to watch the "architecture of the document take shape in the writer's mind" (Bell, 1995, p. 80) Evidently, the shuffling involves grouping, dividing, and sequencing topics, as well as mulling over major issues, such as the thesis, if one is needed.

The nature of the medium does not dictate any particular activities, but encourages certain manipulations—because the individual cards are all pocket size, they are light enough to carry to the library and back, easy to stack, quick to shuffle, small enough to lay out in an array on a table, and compact enough to bundle together with a rubber band, for safekeeping. Of course, the medium also limits the manipulations. The height (three or four inches) restricts the number of topic headings that can be inscribed on any one card, and the width (five or six inches) constrains the number of indented levels. The very chunkiness, so right for an individual notation, becomes a challenge when a student wants to synthesize all the chunks in a pattern. One can stack the cards up in a pile (grouping), order the cards in the pile (sequencing), and one can move groups forward and back, but one is still limited to working with the top levels (the group categories, or the topics within each category). As objects, they retain their individuality, communicating source names and quotes, but where does a particular card fit into its sequence? How is it part of the larger structure? To define that, one can overwrite the top line, with some generalization, and carefully arrange the cards so as to view only these higher level topics, but one sneeze, and the fragile outline is blown apart.

As the student moves from mere grouping and linear sequencing, ideas arise about the meaning of the material, thoughts that are not on the cards, and cannot easily be added to them. Also, the more complex the subject, the more levels one needs, each with meaningful headings summarizing the point of the section. Eventually, when developing a very complicated subject, the piles are not enough, even supplemented with books with yellow stickies poking out of them, and photocopies marked up with highlighters. Although the cards help a student organize the major topics, and may also let one sequence the cards within each pile, they do not allow the student to see, at a glance, any structure below the top level; one has to keep that information in the back of the mind. The student does not yet have a detailed flow, narrative, or argument turning these isolated chunks into a unity, or, as these books sometimes describe it, "a paper" (for instance, Baugh, 1993, p. 58; Lester, 1990, p. 120).

So between the notecards and the final draft one needs an interim, working document—an outline. Offering an overview of multiple levels, and a convenient site in which to develop and modify the structure of a document, the outline emerges from history as a workaday planning device.

MOVING FROM NOTECARDS TO OUTLINES

Generally, the textbook authors who favor notecards also recommend preparing an outline based on them (Andrews & Blickle, 1982 p. 90; Baugh, 1993, p. 58; Johnson, 1992, p. 143; Lester, 1990, p. 120; Pickett, 1984, p. 425; Sandman, Klompus, & Yarrison, 1985, p. 63; Sherman, 1970, p. 49; Sypherd et al., 1957, p. 143; Weidenborner & Caruso, 1990, p. 117.). Weidenborner & Caruso (1990), for instance, portray the outline as a way to get those piles under control:

> No one can tell how many subtopics you will end up with, but you can usually expect to find between ten and twenty groups of cards on the table. In order to come up with a rough outline of the paper, you should consolidate some of the small groups into fairly large ones representing major divisions of the essay. (p. 114)

> An outline of some sort is essential if you hope to control all the information that lies spread out on the table in front of you. Outlining can be done in several stages, culminating in a detailed plan for the paper, in which each note card has been assigned to a specific point in the outline. (p. 117)

So the first phase of outlining is actually to manipulate the cards a few more times. The outline, in this view, is a simple recording of the final order of the cards.

However, other textbook authors recognize that creating the outline may involve more than transcribing the grouping and sequencing of note cards, so there has to be more give and take between the outline and the notes. Marckwardt & Cassidy (1960) see the outline as helping direct the actual research, and being improved by what a student learns while reading:

> The advantage of making your outline early is that it will guide you in reading and note taking. You may find that in some division of your subject you need to read further. It also gives you a pattern by which to sort your notes. Keep enlarging and improving your outline with all necessary subdivisions until you have finished your reading. Then go over it carefully and correct any inconsistencies or faults of structure. Decide what details you will use and discard the others. (p. 410)

Similarly, Weisman (1962) argues that the outline "permits the investigator to test the adequacy of his data" (p. 261), suggesting the author compare the information on the paper outline with the notes on the cards.

Sherman (1970) recognizes that the outline may take the organization beyond that seen in the cards, and tells students to "Rearrange your note-cards according to the final outline" (p. 44). In 1989 Samuels suggests transporting the subject headings from the first outline onto the notes, sorting the cards according to those headings, and then rereading each pile in order to "determine the overall significance of your research" (pp. 58-59), coming to conclusions that may, in turn, change the outline itself. So do Weidenborner and Caruso (1990, p. 114). As Johnson (1992) says, "As you sort your cards, notice how the material helps you to create an outline at the same time that the outline helps you to shape your material....It's a back-and-forth operation" (p. 143). Alred, Oliu, and Brusaw (1992), who quite forthrightly argue in one place that a student should complete all research before outlining, admit that the outline itself may reveal places "where more research is necessary before you begin to write the draft" (p. 111). Rubens (1992), who also argues for outlining as a stage that must be completed before drafting, sees a similar benefit in regard to research when the outline "reveals missing information and other obstacles" (p. 17). And Houp, Pearsall, and Tebeaux (1995) approach the matter cautiously, declaring that a writer should not actually do outlining while discovering thoughts and studying the subject, but, at least, use "familiar arrangement patterns as aids in discovering your material" (p. 22).

So, a few of the textbook authors who sometimes describe a series of discrete stages (researching, then outlining, then writing) recognize an intellectual benefit to comparing the paper outline with the note cards, to bring both into synchronicity. But the physical pieces of paper prevent complete synthesis.

Pickett and Laster (1984), for instance, urge students to go back from the formal outline and "mark each note card with a Roman numeral, letter of the alphabet, or Arabic numeral to show to what section or subsection of the outline the note card corresponds. Then rearrange the note cards accordingly" (p. 425). Sandman, Klampus, and Yarrison (1985) give the same advice (p. 63).

This recommendation (surely ignored by all but the most obedient students) points to a major problem with notecards and paper as media. Having created an outline on standard 8.5"x11" or 8.5"x14" writing paper, the writer cannot easily make clear the relationship between a particular outline heading and a specific group of 3"x5" or 4"x6" note cards. How can the writer make the connection between the heading in the outline and the right pile of notecards? Of course, the writer could draw a mental arrow from the outline sheet to the pile of cards, or scribble code numbers from the outline on the individual cards, but in either case, the cross-referencing between outline and note remains tenuous, a challenge to memory. The information does not appear in a single document.

Underneath such discussions is a fundamental assumption: that the outline, logically connected to the notes, will remain physically separate, a document visibly distinct from the notes. And the draft, although based on the outline, must become yet another discrete document. To people who spend most of their days using pencil and paper, this concept seems "obvious." In effect, the paper medium has suggested or re-enforced an idea of notes and outline as discrete entities, rather than as, say, two views of the same material. (By contrast, a single electronic outline can contain headings, with notes folded underneath them, to be viewed when necessary, or hidden, and one can write the draft using the same outline, viewed in word processing mode, so that, in reality, all three aspects of the material appear in the same document).

From Discrete Documents to Discrete Stages

Perhaps working from the media-influenced assumption that notes and the outline must be physically discrete entities, a large group of the textbook authors—stretching from the 1940s to the 1990s—tend to portray creation itself as a sequence of discrete steps or stages, each resulting in its own document. First one makes an outline, then one writes a draft; once one has completed the outline, one moves to the next step, and, if one has further thoughts about structure, one incorporates those in the draft, rather than going back to the outline.[2]

Some textbook authors envision only a few stages, some as many as nine (Perrin, 1955, p. 5). A few explicitly use the term *stages* (Alred, et al., 1992, p. 112; Baugh, 1993, p. 58; Johnson, 1992, p. 133; Perrin, 1955, p. 5; Santmyers, 1949, p. 24), some refer to *steps* (Alred et al., 1992, p. 112; Ehrlich & Murphy, 1964, p. 28; Lester, 1990, p. 123; Myers, 1955, p. 258; Santmyers, 1949, p. 24; Sypherd et al., 1957, p. 148; Trzyna & Batschelet, 1987, pp. 98, 107; Wilcox, 1977, p. 84), but most simply draw sharp distinctions in terms such as "before" (Hacker & Renshaw, 1979, p. 102; Lester, 1990, p. 120; Rubens, 1992, p. 16; Sherman, 1955, p. 9) and "afterward" (Fowler et al., 1992, p. 38; Smart & Lang, 1943, p. 27) or "finishing" (Houp et al., 1995, p. 25) the "completed" (Baugh, 1993, p. 67; Ehrlich & Murphy, 1964, p. 28) outline before beginning the draft. Often the phases are numbered, to emphasize the sequential nature of the stages. In the most common model, the research stage yields the note cards, the planning stage ends in an outline, the drafting stage comes up with a first draft, and the revision stage produces a final version.

Warriner and colleagues (1950, 1958) articulated this separation of the writing process into distinct stages in his famous handbook:

> In practice, as you know from your own experience, a writer begins with a general plan and ends with details of wording, sentence structure and grammar. First he chooses the subject of his composition. Second, he tackles the preparation of this material, from rough ideas to final outline. Third, he undertakes the writing itself, once again beginning with a rough form (the first draft) and ending with a finished form (the final draft) that is as nearly perfect as he can make it. (p. 11)

How plausible this sounds, when not examined carefully. How sensible! How untrue. Even Warriner must have recognized that in general students tend to take notes, organize, and write, in fits and starts, now doing one activity, now another.

Emig (1971) struck an important blow against this odd separation of structuring and drafting, by pointing out that none of the 16 professional and academic writers she interviewed did what the textbooks said was standard practice. Emig says:

The data from the questionnaire also suggest that a second generalization of rhetoric texts and manuals about planning is not valid, at least for this sample of writers—that is, all planning precedes all writing as all writing precedes all revising. The metaphor implied in these accounts about the writing process is linear: each "stage" is monolithic, and holds a fixed position in a lock-step chronological process. There are, in other words, no major recursive features in the writing process....Clearly, for these authors the so-called "stages" of writing are not fixed in an inexorable sequence. Rather, they occur and reoccur throughout the process. These data then make suspect the straight line which rhetoric texts imply as an appropriate metaphor for the writing process. (p. 67)

The work of Emig (1971), Flower and Hayes (1981a, 1981b, 1984), and Flower et al. (1990), among others, led theorists to view writing as "a dynamic multistep process that involves discovering ideas as we think and even as we write" (Daiute, 1985, p. 65).

Despite this new line of thinking, however, some textbook authors continued to talk as if all research could end when one starts the outline, and all thinking about structure and thesis could come to a halt when one stops outlining and starts an entirely new activity, known as drafting.

Of course, this model does not derive simply from the media used. Pedagogy may be another force driving the textbook authors to talk about outlining as one step, drafting as another. Sorting the work of creation into stages makes for neater syllabi, more clearly distinguished sections in the book, and more convenient teaching, because one can discuss each activity separately, and assign different documents as exercises. Santmyers (1949) justifies his stages in this way: "Because the four stages have their own techniques and activities, you can consider and think about each in order, separately and purposefully" (p. 26). Perrin (1955) believes that dividing the work up into stages may also simplify the actual work:

Writing a paper can be divided for convenience of discussion into nine stages...The problems of all the stages attempted together are enough to swamp anyone, even a professional writer, but if one step is undertaken at a time and disposed of, an orderly, workmanlike process can replace the jumble of worries. (p. 5)

Stages seem reasonable, at first glance. For instance, Alred and colleagues (1992) argue that you cannot do an outline when you know little about the subject. "You should not try to create your outline until you have completed your research and recorded all your notes, of course, because until then you will not know enough about your subject to be able to create a good outline" (p. 111). This argument, though, ignores the fact that writers accumulate ideas and facts gradually, and during that time, the writers need to keep thinking about their goals, and therefore, the structure of their material.

Talking about stages as if writers must finish one to move on to the next, and as if each stage yields a single definite document that is never again modified, gives a false idea of the way real people write, a model that may, in part, be based on what people saw when notes were on cards, and outlines on paper.

However, the stages model is undermined, in many of these same textbooks, by the actual tasks the authors assign students to perform, when creating the outline. At the very least, these activities require so many revisions of the outline, so many iterations, that students would have to emerge with a series of outlines, not just one. And some authors recognize that outlining may take place side by side with writing and revising, thus fuzzing the edges of the stages even more.

What Happens During Outlining, Then?

Whether the authors present outlining as a stage, or an ongoing process that interacts with other activities such as research, writing, and revision, most textbook authors give students some general guidelines on what to do when outlining, while acting as if the detailed activities are well-known to their readers, and need not be discussed in much depth. Individually, most authors only mention three or four particular activities the student might do to create an outline. But collectively, the textbook authors' recommendations add up to almost the same set of activities as we saw with electronic outlining—with three significant differences: These authors leave out any note-taking and research, as separate activities operating on separate documents; add a distinctive emphasis on one kind of outline (for an essay); and do not consider drafting part of outlining. The activities that are mentioned include the following (with some representative citations in notes):

- Making a list of topics[3]
- Adding or deleting topics[4]
- Moving topics from place to place[5]
- Eliminating duplicate topics and specifically making sure that a topic does not appear as a subtopic under itself[6]
- Classifying or grouping related topics[7]
- Dividing one topic into its component subtopics[8]
- Subordinating some topics to others[9]
- Sequencing[10]
- Confirming completeness, by checking to make sure you have not left out anything important in your notes[11]

- Making the text of related headings consistent[12]
- Working on one layer at a time[13]
- Making the outline match the structure of an essay, by including an introduction,[14] starting with a thesis statement,[15] ensuring that the headings support the thesis,[16] including a conclusion,[17] and adopting a consistent point of view[18]
- Double-checking to make sure you have done these activities correctly[19]

These activities may operate on various documents, from scratch notes (Leggett et al., 1991, p. 359; Perrin, 1955, p. 13; Warriner et al., 1958, p. 11), trees (Leggett et al., 1991, pp. 359, 365) and nonlinear outlines for brainstorming (Andrews & Blickle, 1982, p. 88; Rubens,1992, p. 19) through simple lists (Alred et al., 1992, p. 113; Leggett et al., 1991, p. 359; Mansfield & Bahniuk, 1981, p. 268; Markel, 1984, p. 69; Mills & Walter, 1978, p. 68; Wilcox, 1977, p. 84), numbered lists (Pickett & Laster, 1984, p. 118; Weisman, 1962, p. 261), a preliminary outline (Alvarez, 1980, p. 157; Andrews & Blickle, 1982, p. 88; Hacker, 1994, p. 27; Sandman et al., 1985, p. 63; Sherman, 1970, p. 48; Trzyna & Batschelet, 1987, p. 102), and working outline (Alred et al., 1992, p. 113; Alvarez, 1980, p. 176; Hacker, 1994, p. 27; Leggett et al., 1991, p. 359), which may itself take the form of a topic outline (Alred et al., 1992, p. 113; Mills & Walter, 1978, p. 55; Pickett & Laster, 1984, p. 118), sentence outline (Mills & Walter, 1978, p. 55; Pickett & Laster, 1984, p. 118; Sandman et al., 1985, p. 65), or paragraph outline (Mills & Walter, 1978, p. 55; Samuels, 1989, p. 72). The proliferation of distinct documents, across the spectrum of textbooks, suggests a common model, that is, one that envisions a series of distinct physical entities.

Very few textbook authors like to admit how many, many versions the students would have to go through to do a thorough job. I believe that the authors who stress revising or re-checking the outline move students a lot closer to the reality they face. Those who mention a series of outlines (such as a simple list, a topic outline, a formal outline) also communicate the idea that outlining itself means working with a series of documents.

Most writers will probably have to make many passes through the material, doing different activities on each pass (not even one activity per pass!), looping back, jumping here and there, redoing and undoing, as they develop the outline, and, when they are using paper, they will probably have to make several copies of the outline. Thus, Wilcox (1977) actually warns the students that they will probably not get away with a single outline (as document), "Write a working outline. This is the outline from which you actually write. Since often it must be revised several times, it would be more accurate to say 'outlines.'" (p. 84)

Trzyna & Batschelet (1987) recommend "multiple outlines" (p. 102). And more than 20 other authors admit, or suggest, or forthrightly announce that students may often have to make more than one version of "the" outline.[20]

All this creation and revision; all this to-and-fro, combined with the mutual interplay of research and planning; all these versions of the emerging outline suggest a dynamic, recursive, interlocking set of activities. How could they really be carried out in a series of neat stages, as in a factory turning out tin cans? No matter what sequence an author might use to list these activities, the student cannot hope to walk through them as a neat sequence of steps in a procedure. As Markel (1984) says, "The human mind is not so structured or orderly" (p. 69).

Mills and Walter (1978), who spend more than 30 pages explaining how to organize an outline logically, point out that students cannot expect to proceed step by step directly to an organized outline, because the mind doesn't work that way, but has what we would today call a fuzzy logic:

> It is hard to discuss the subject without implying one idea that is actually ridiculous. This ridiculous idea is that the minds of intelligent people work in an orderly process just as an outline is developed. Nothing could be further from the truth. Of course the purpose of an outline is to establish an orderly relationship among a group of facts or ideas. And intelligence could almost be defined as the ability to perceive relationships. Nevertheless, intelligent thought processes appear to be infinitely more complex and more varied in structure than is even remotely implied in the concept of an outline. (p. 67)

But the paper medium makes changing a single outline difficult, messy, and unappetizing (Smith, 1990). Handwriting an outline does not encourage constant reorganization. It's hard enough to get the ideas down once. To make a change, one has to erase and rewrite, or draw circles around a passage and add an arrow pointing to its new location, cross out a dud section, or scribble in a new one in very small text so that one can fit it between two lines. However, this exploding outline, with stars, cross-hatchings, additions, and deletions, quickly becomes difficult to read. What started as a way of considering alternate structures quickly gets too complicated to figure out. Instead of emerging with a high-level overview that one can scan through for patterns, one gets a mess, and to decipher it, one has to descend to the level of words and arrows, and follow the material sequentially.

Of course, one can copy the entire outline over, making the changes as one goes, which means writing the same headings over and over, just in a different order. But handwriting is never easy, and the task of copying the same text over and over, even if in slightly different order, is enough to drive many people to rebellion (Daiute, 1985, pp. 36-7).

The medium of paper, then, is adequate when all a student must do is dash off a single, instantly perfect outline, or even two, but resistant when a person must continuously reconsider the organization, as with a large, complex topic—but such reconsideration is a major reason these text-book authors recommend making an outline in the first place. The text-book authors, then, are asking for students to rethink their structures in many passes, but not saying how to handle the changes on paper. What remains unacknowledged is the difficulty placed in the students' way by the medium. The textbooks put students in a double bind: They must make changes to the outline in order to define the most effective struc-ture, but they must use paper, which militates against their making very many significant changes.

The Emphasis on Product

The dilemma these authors put their readers in, then, resembles the con-fusion caused by teachers who overemphasize the final product. To hear theorists tell the story, composition instructors during the 1950s focused so intently on the product that they gave beginners the impression that anyone ought to be able to compose a complete outline in a single sitting, and then write a perfect final draft just as simply. Daiute (1985) shows how this product orientation may have been reinforced by the recalci-trance of the paper medium:

> Unfortunately, this focus on the end product often gives beginners the idea that writers always compose good texts....The emphasis on writing as a static product may have come about, in part, because the traditional writing instruments and surfaces do not allow writers to change the page easily. Thus, writers have a physical stake in producing final products on the first try because revising and even minor editing involve recopying. (pp. 52-53)

Such a feat—producing a perfect outline or essay in one try—involves so many complex and overlapping activities that even the most experi-enced writers would have trouble managing the juggling act.

Here's one reason, I suspect, that students have come to hate outlining, at least in its purest paper form, considering it "the unpleasant assign-ment" (Santmyers, 1949, p. 43), or "an unreasonable imposition...an extra task" (Myers, 1955, pp. 257-258).

And perhaps sensing some of that resentment, some teachers came to encourage students by promising that they could stop working on the outline as soon as they started writing. As teachers, they probably understood how exasperating it could be to make real revisions to any outline, so as textbook authors they implied that there was a complete separation between the outline work and the writing of the draft—a separation modeled by the fact that on paper, these are different documents. Just get through the outline, they pleaded, and then you can let that sit, while you write the draft. "After the outline is completed, the writer is ready for the actual writing of the article," which consists of "filling in the outline" with details, say Smart and Lang (1943, p. 27). "If you write a good enough outline, you don't have to do much more than copy to get your final paper," claims Myers (1955, p. 258). Baugh (1993) says encouragingly: "All you have left to do is fill in the words for each main point, one paragraph at a time" (p. 67).

Writing as Part of Outlining

Most of the group of textbook authors who describe writing in terms of stages draw a sharp distinction between outlining and writing. Smart and Lang (1943) set the tone: "After the outline is completed, the writer is ready for the actual writing of the article" (p. 27). Warriner and colleagues (1958) say that in the third step the writer undertakes "the writing itself" (p. 11). Dietrich and Brooks (1958) dismiss the idea of writing as an active part of outlining: "The emphasis in every outline is on ideas, not on phraseology" (p.110).

However, instead of making such a clean separation between the outline stage and the drafting stage, a few—very few—of the textbook authors recognize that as writers outline they are working with words, and, just to articulate the structure, they must write. For instance, Myers (1955) says, "If you write a good enough outline, you don't have to do much more than copy to get your final paper" (p. 258). Note the difficulty that Perrin (1955), a stages theorist, tries to overcome when he admits "Of course some writing has been going on in the last three steps, but actual consecutive writing ordinarily takes place as the sixth step in developing a paper" (p. 15).

Certainly, the writing of headings and subheadings involves shorter, more concentrated chunks than discursive writing does, but if the headings are to communicate to the reader, they must be written with the care we give to a maxim, or title. Mills and Walter (1978) argue that some headings are just placeholders, that is, "signals to write" (p. 65), but point out that other headings act as potential titles for sections, and must therefore convey the contents adroitly to the reader. Weiss (1982), too, stresses that the headings need to be made "persuasive...instead of the usual uncommunicative noun strings (categorical or topical)" (p. 59). "The first improvement, changing the headings from dull and descriptive to thematic and evocative, is a basic journalist technique. Actually, it involves turning headings into headlines" (p. 60).

In a backhanded way, Sandman and colleagues (1985) also recognize how much writing is involved in a thorough outline, arguing that if one is going to do all that writing in an outline, one might as well do it in the first draft, instead. "In truth, however, though virtually all good writers use some kind of outline, few people spend the time and effort it takes to write a formal one, because it takes nearly as much time to write a sentence outline as it takes to write a first draft" (p. 65).

The most straightforward recognition of the value of the outline as writing comes from journalist Tom Wolfe, quoted by Hacker (1994): "By writing an outline you really are writing in a way, because you're creating the structure of what you're going to do. Once I really know what I'm going to write, I don't find the actual writing takes all that long" (p. 36).

That's been my experience, too. However, most people continue to think of an outline as just a kind of aid to memory, not "real writing," and so they scribble the headings with no sense of the reader, including instructions to themselves ("Put Doggett material here."), or making dummy headings, with the understanding that they can be fixed later. In this way, much of the value of outlining is lost.

In fact, the only "writing" activity these authors generally recommend during outlining is to impose parallel structure on all headings. Usually, this activity means converting all headings of the same level in the same section to the same grammatical form. Many textbook authors just insist on the student carrying out this action without giving any rationale. Most of those who do provide an explanation stress structural logic:

1. All the headings have the same importance, and are at the same level in the hierarchy, so, logically, they should be parallel in grammatical form (Elsbree & Bracher, 1967, p. 40; Leggett et al., 1960, p. 201; Pickett & Laster, 1984, p. 118; Sypherd et al., 1957, p. 144; Wicker & Albrecht, 1960, p. 58).
2. A single principle must be applied to divide a topic into a set of components, and parallel format proves one has done so methodically. As Jordan (1965) says, "You cannot alternatively file your correspondence chronologically by date of writing and alphabetically by addressee" (p. 109). (Compare Shelton, 1995, p. 41).

A few other authors argue for parallelism rhetorically, saying it will ensure that the reader can see the headings all belong in the same group, and can then compare them easily, with little extra thought required. As Sherman (1955) says, "Such a practice enables a reader to become familiar with the pattern and hence to read more efficiently" (p. 14).

However, because the textbooks offer so little real advice on how to write meaningful, persuasive headings, we may conclude that most authors still, unconsciously, have not recognized the degree to which an outline can actually become the document itself. Once a writer uses electronic outlining, this transformation becomes easy; and the point these few authors bring up becomes obvious—that every ounce of writing one does in the outline can move the emerging document forward.

Dealing With New Ideas That Come Up As One Writes

Because so many textbook authors conceive of outlining as the culmination of all planning, and consider drafting as a simple matter of carrying out the plan, they often overlook the fact that people come up with new ideas as they write.

In the traditional theory, there is a simple relationship between outline and draft, expressed in metaphors such as the blueprint and the map. The writer just has to follow the outline without deviating from its path; one need not expect to learn anything new as one writes. Evidently, encouraged by the idea of pure stages, many classroom teachers over the years have frightened their students into near paralysis by insisting that the outline exactly match the final draft. No unexpected ideas should creep in, nothing should be discovered, no detours explored, no life arise during writing.

In those circumstances, many students emerged from English classes hating the outline as a dead hand. "Some will warn you that the outline will make your writing wooden, lifeless, or at best the mere thumping of a treadmill" (Santmyers, 1949, p. 43). Rose (1980) found that many students who were blocked were just trying to work within a set of rigid rules, in this way.

Recognizing that many high school teachers had made students think of the outline as a straitjacket, limiting their future movement, several textbook authors admitted that the outline might not, in fact, foresee all possible ideas or structures. As early as 1949, Thomas stressed elasticity, allowing students a little give and take before the outline snapped them back in line. "The fact is that the outline serves as a place of departure and return during actual composition" (p. 140). He recognized that the writer might need to defer, add, or combine points for emphasis or suspense, insert an illustration, make a transition, or put in an introductory remark, but he still saw the outline as a useful form of control for the writer.

He may purposively take by-paths but he does not wander in a maze. As a rule, radical divergence from the general scheme shown in the outline is neither necessary nor desirable. If a paper drifts away from the basic plan, probably there are logical flaws, in either the outline or the composition—or very likely, in both. ... No matter how much variance is permitted in detail, the following test of over-all content always is valid: *Nothing in the outline should fail to be presented in the composition; conversely, no essential topic or major body of material in the composition should fail to be indicated in the outline.* (pp. 140-141)

Student reaction over the last 50 years has often been to write the outline after the composition—completely avoiding any possible benefit from outlining, but fulfilling the requirement for a one-to-one match between outline and draft, quite neatly. Thomas (1949) complains: "Students who first write their own papers without method and afterwards attempt to outline them, 'because we have to turn in an outline,' usually are simply wasting time, paper, and energy—not to mention the patience of their instructors" (p. 130).

Elsbree and Bracher (1967) acknowledge that students often fake outlining, putting one together after their draft, but the authors try to shame the students into writing the outline first. "The student who hurriedly makes one up after writing the paper usually cheats himself more than he does the instructor" (pp. 30-31).

Elsbree and Bracher (1967) do not take a severe attitude, though, because they envision students veering away from their outlines during drafts, and encourage that: "Try regarding your outline as a guide to your structure and plan, not as a fixed commitment. If, while writing, you discover necessary changes, feel free to make them in the outline and the composition" (p. 45).

In the 1980s we get even more mellow advice, encouraging students to wander away from their outline, if they need to. Alvarez (1980) says:

Don't be afraid to deviate from your outline as you write. The shape of a piece, scientist Gregory Bateson reminds us, "sometimes emerges out of a sort of wrestling process." So rather than hang on to a plan that no longer reflects reality, go with the flow of the piece as it develops. Most of us learn as we write—one of the prime benefits of writing. (p. 177)

Similarly, Markel (1984) says:

Few people are able to create a perfect outline—either public or private. With private outlines, you will find that as you write your first draft, you have forgotten something or that something in the outline isn't relevant and has to be dropped. This doesn't mean that the whole outline is flawed;

it simply means that you never know what you really want to say until you try to put it on paper. Writing forces you to examine your ideas. (p. 68)

The new freedom extends into the 90s, with Bell (1995, p. 100), Brusaw and colleagues (1993, p. 485), Fowler and colleagues (1992, p. 43), and Leggett and colleagues (1991, pp. 365-366). For instance, Bell (1995) quotes a Bob Velasquez on the outline as a general (but not strict) guide: "No matter how carefully I outline my material in advance, I always seem to discover new possibilities or interesting side roads as I write. It doesn't make sense to exclude good ideas just because they didn't appear in an original outline. So I try to use my outline as a general guide to writing, not as a fixed agenda of points and subpoints" (p. 100).

We might characterize this emerging approach as soft outlining. One develops a structure with the outline, but leaves the outline behind as one writes the draft itself. So even among people who live with word processing, the idea persists that an outline and a draft must be separate documents, and there is no explicit recognition that a writer can have multiple views (page layout, normal, outline) of the same emerging draft.

A second approach toward handling ideas that come up during writing is to revise the outline as a working model of the structure of the document. Thomas (1949), for instance, suggests a sentence outline during research, a perfected version before writing—and revisions "during the actual writing of the paper, should new interpretations occur or new material be discovered" (p. 131).

Hammond and Allen (1953) reassure their readers that "The outline does not 'set' the report, in the sense of imposing a rigid immutable form upon it, for the outline itself is not rigid. It may be changed if necessary" (p. 59). If a valuable idea occurs to the writer during the writing, what should be done? Hammond and Allen show why the writer should incorporate the idea into the outline before going on:

> If the writer is not using an outline, he may choose one of three courses: (1) He may insert the idea into whatever portion he happened to be writing when it occurred to him, which may or may not be the most effective position. This is what usually happens. (2) He may try to file the idea away in his mind for use in an appropriate context. This course is distracting and uncertain of fulfillment. (3) He may simply drop the idea altogether. None of these courses is really satisfactory. On the other hand, if the writer to whom a useful idea occurs is working from an outline, all he has to do is refer the idea to the outline, discover the most pertinent, effective place for it, and incorporate it into his plan.(p. 59)

Perrin (1955) agrees: "But it is necessary to remember that a paper cannot always be completely visualized ahead of writing, that any preliminary outline is a working plan—the best way you can see to lay out the material before you begin to write. Even the most perfectly numbered outline should be changed in the process of writing if there is good reason to change it" (p. 15).

Pickett and Laster (1984) envision the revising process involving "several drafts of the outline and the report" (p. 426). Johnson (1992) sees such revisions taking placing during the first draft (p. 141); Fowler and colleagues (1992) encourage students to revise the outline "no matter when it's made" (p. 35), even after the draft. Hacker (1994) offers a significant qualification of her approach to stages when she acknowledges that students may need to circle back to revise their outline:

> Of course the writing process will not always occur for you quite as simply as just described. While drafting, for example, you may discover an interesting new approach to your topic that demands a revised plan. Or while revising you may need to generate more ideas and draft new material. Although you should generally move from planning to drafting to revising, be prepared to circle back to earlier stages whenever the need arises. (p. 2)

Houp and colleagues (1995) make the strongest current statement on behalf of revising the outline as you discover ideas during writing:

> Discovery does not stop when you begin to write. The reverse is usually true. For most people, writing stimulates discovery. Writing clarifies your thoughts, refines your ideas, and leads you to new connections. Therefore, be flexible. Be willing to revise your plan to accommodate new insights as they occur. (p. 28)

This approach—taking new ideas that come up during writing, and incorporating them into the outline—requires defacing the clean paper outline with added scribbles, lines, and arrows, or recopying the whole with additions. Of course, if one were working on an electronic document, one could switch from word processing to outlining in a moment, make the modification, then return to discursive prose. When an outline is simply one view of a document, the switch between word processing and outlining becomes a fast way to pursue a sudden realization, placing a note about it in the right place, and returning to the original task quickly enough to pick up where you left off. In this sense, electronic outlining is a visible exemplum of the approach recommended by this second group of textbook authors, even though they themselves do not urge students to do the revisions electronically. It's interesting, though, that after the writers of the 1940s and early 1950s, we have to wait for the era of word processing for textbook authors to talk this way again. And even these authors do not start from the assumption that all work should be done electronically.

Revising a Draft With an Eye to Structure

In the traditional view, once a writer has completed a draft, any revision—even changes in structure—should take place in the draft, not the outline. Thus, when one realizes that the structure isn't quite right after writing a draft, one leaves the old outline untouched, having moved beyond that stage. Now any modifications to the structure should be applied to the draft (Alvarez,1980, p.177; Bell, 1995, p. 100; Brusaw et al., 1993, p. 485; Fowler et al., 1992, p. 43; Markel, 1984, p. 68; Thomas, 1949, p. 140). Perhaps the difficulty of going back and changing the outline, when it is on paper, convinced the text book authors to fit any new ideas into the draft, rather than going back and revising the outline to incorporate them in a new structure.

Hacker and Renshaw (1979), for instance, envision students "reshaping" the draft with numbers, arrows, scissors, and tape, "possibly moving paragraphs and sentences about" (pp. 102, 109). Crews (1980) points to the practice of professional writers when he stresses the importance of making major structural changes, as opposed to what Sommers (1980) calls "rewording activity," but he too sees the site of revision as the draft.

A few authors do encourage students to create an outline of their draft, to be able to see its structure clearly, when revising, but these outlines are not modifications of the original outline—they are new. Martin (1957) sees a new outline as "a tool for reorganizing what has already been composed" (pp. 139-140), particularly after a writer has written "without preliminary concern for neat and efficient order" (p. 140). Sypherd and colleagues (1957) recognize that students may be required to hand in an outline along with the draft, but, even if they don't have to, Sypherd and colleagues argue that students ought to revise the outline "to conform to the paper" because it will help the students check over the document for "gaps in information or development of thought" (p. 149). Elsbree and Bracher (1967), who have already encouraged students to deviate from their outlines in writing the draft, suggest "outlining the defective structure of the composition" as a way of diagnosing what has gone wrong. "Used diagnostically, the formal outline can reveal the particular failures in plan and structure" (p. 31). The original outline, then, has been left behind, and the writer is looking at an entirely new one, pulled together by rereading the draft itself.

In the 1980s, textbook authors begin to reflect contemporary research on how real people actually write (such as Emig, 1971 and Sommers, 1980, summarized in Nystrand, Greene, & Wiemelt, 1993, pp. 280-283).

This research shows that professional writers usually start revising a draft by working at a global level on content and structure, before descending to words, phrases, and sentences. Coe (1981) urges confused students to clarify the structure of a jumbled first draft by creating an outline of what has already been written, in order to consider its organization, free of the details. He tells students that they ought to act like "experienced writers" and focus first on structure. How to spot the structure in the draft? Make a new outline, diagnosing the structure inherent in that draft:

> One of the clearest distinctions between experienced and inexperienced writers is that inexperienced writers rarely reorder. Inexperienced writers add, delete, and substitute, but they rarely reorder. Thus there is a whole type of revision that inexperienced writers typically do not even consider. That type of revision is concerned with structure—logic, organization, and development—and is often the key to successful writing, especially in academic and professional contexts....In order to revise the structure of a piece of writing, you must see it. This is often difficult, especially with longer writings. The basic structure can get lost under a mass of details. The solution is to make an outline of what is already written. (p. 91)

Hacker (1994) suggests that "a formal outline may be useful later in the writing process, after you have written a rough draft, especially if your subject matter is complex" (p. 27). After a complete first draft is written, she too stresses that students ought to make "global improvements" rather than "moving words around" (p. 40). But before restructuring the draft, students might want to "consider sketching a revised outline" (p. 46).

This diagnostic use of a new outline suggests how valuable outlining can be for analyzing and understanding a text. Of course, if one is working electronically, one can move a heading—and its attached paragraphs—from one place to another, in a few seconds. Instead of having to discern the structure through a haze of words, one already has the structure visible or can switch to outline view, and, if one decides to change the structure, one can do so without creating a second document to reflect the first.

Once again, the textbooks present a world dominated by the paper-based idea that writers create a series of separate documents—the notes, the outline, the draft, and now, the second outline. In many ways, then, the intractability of paper may have contributed to the idea that an outline must be one document, and the draft another. And, since there are two distinct products, the idea naturally arose that writers create them in two distinct stages.

Ideas often outlast the media environments and technologies that spawned them. But, the uncritical attitude most of these textbook authors show toward paper leads some of them to gloss over its drawbacks, and sketch a misleading picture of a sequence of creative stages, as if they really exist, or should, each neatly producing a distinct document.

We can get a sense of the persistence of this mental model when we look at the way it resisted acknowledging the arrival of another machine for writing— the typewriter. How much did that change ideas of outlining?

THE ADVENT OF THE TYPEWRITER

By the 1960s we begin to hear a few textbooks talk of students using typewriters, which made drafting and recopying faster for some students, and slower for others (Ehrlich & Murphy, 1964, p. 37; Harwell, 1960, p. 120; Wicker & Albrecht, 1960, p. 59). First released commercially in 1874, the typewriter had gradually taken over offices by the turn of the century, when secretaries organized the Typewriters' Union (Bliven, 1954, p. 77). Typewriters then infiltrated newspapers, and became cheap mass-production office machines by the mid-1950s, with 3.5 million professional typists (Bliven, 1954, p. 229). By the 1960s most college students were using typewriters extensively.

Ehrlich and Murphy (1964) sketch the scene as the writer sits down to work:

> The writer gets ready for drafting his research paper by arranging all the tools he will need throughout his work: The outline is on the desk before him, along with paper, pencils, and typewriter. Desk dictionary, writing handbook, and thesaurus, or other word books are available, but beyond arm's length, preferably across the room from the student's desk. Nothing else is needed or desirable. (p. 37)

The media are the same: ink on paper. But the tool is different. What advantages did these authors see in typing an outline? Neatness, mostly. With a typewriter, Wicker and Albrecht (1960) can specify that each new level should be indented "five spaces further in" (p. 59). Of the few authors who explicitly mention typewriting, only Harwell (1960) sees the typewriter as an opportunity for new formatting. Daringly, he suggests that students handle first-level heads this way: "Centered between margins, written in all-capitals, underlined. Three blank lines above, two below. No punctuation follows" (p. 120). (Compare Schriver, 1997, on the "unattractive conventions" imposed by the typewriter, p. 40). Ugly as this formatting now seems to us, it at least took advantage of the typewriter as a tool, to emphasize the importance of these major headings.

In general, then, the typewriter may have made the text clearer and easier to read than handwritten copy, but, at least for these authors, it did not suggest any new methods of articulating the outline structure in visual form. (In an office, a writer could change ribbon colors or type balls, but no textbook mentions these additional possibilities, probably because they were expensive, dirty, and time-consuming to perform.) In addition, for students who could touch type, the machine may have made the labor of recopying one outline with changes, to create a new one, somewhat less tedious than before, when working with pen and paper. But then, if one sees an outline as a one-shot document to be discarded after drafting, why would anyone care to make it easier to revise?

After the 1960s, most authors do not make specific mention of typewriting, but talk as if a writer could do exactly the same work with a pen, pencil, or typewriter. Why this silence on the effect of a new tool? Some reticence may be due to the fact that certain students could not afford typewriters, and the authors did not want to make these students feel like second-class citizens. The authors do not show much sensitivity to media, evidently thinking that an outline is an outline, whether one makes it with a pen or a typewriter. Also, the typewriter had already appeared on the scene long before Marshall McLuhan (1962, 1964a, 1964b) and theorists of the 1960s spotlighted the importance of media, focusing on TV. As Tuman (1992) points out there are very few historical studies of the typewriter, most in the business libraries (p. 1).

In the 1950s typing was considered the domain of the clerical underclass. Bliven's (1953) book on the history of the typewriter begins with a long chapter about secretaries. Tuman (1992) finds a similar class bias when he reviews what the Harbrace Handbook of 1986 has to say about typing:

> A work designed for profession-bound college students, those intended to create or author, rather than merely reproduce texts, [it] barely touches on the larger issue of manuscript preparation, devoting a scant nine pages (out of over 500) to the topic, with only a single six-sentence paragraph devoted to the issue of typing. This section, entitled "Legible Typing", includes directions about checking the quality of the ribbon and the type, double-spacing, and not overstriking to make corrections. (p. 2)

However, Tuman (1992) believes that some of this contempt for media analysis, at least as far as the typewriter is concerned, was justified, because typing had so little to do with the making of an original thought. For modern literacy, with its focus on the individual mind producing an essay full of critical insight, the typewriter was simply a device for producing clean copy, so, Tuman argues, the textbook authors and professors mentioned typing only to urge students to cross out irrelevancies on the page.

> Behind this advice lies the basic assumption of higher literacy instruction embedded in college-level composition and literature classes—that what we mean by writing has little to do with the transcription of letters and far more to do with the ability to create a text containing original thought. Typing has had such little impact on this higher-level literacy over the last 120 years precisely because it is not perceived as having anything substantial to do with literacy, that is, with creating or comprehending the content, rather than the physical form, of texts. Why should we expect so much more from computers?...Are computers really anything more than turbo-charged typewriters? (p. 2)

On the other hand, many writers found that the keyboard offered a faster way to get their thoughts from mind to paper than the pen or pencil. Daiute (1985) points out that we can talk faster than we can write with a pen, so "speakers do not have to hold their ideas in mind as long as writers do before they can express themselves" (p. 53). The person using a pen therefore had to do more mental juggling, in short-term memory. Touch typing meant one's fingers could move almost as quickly as one's thoughts, removing the delays and hand pain involved with using a pen or pencil, allowing the ideas to pour out unchecked (Daiute, 1985, pp. 30-32).

Even when they give a nod to typing, the textbook authors don't mention convenience, class, or the possibilities for alternate formatting of a typed outline, despite evidence from research such as that of Burtis, Bereiter, Scardamalia, and Tetroe (1983); Haas (1989a, 1989b, summarized in 1996), Haas and Hayes (1986), and Scardamalia and Bereiter (1983) indicating that there are real advantages in technologies that "enable writing to proceed more quickly, and that generate more legible text." (Schriver, 1997, p. 36). Their indifference suggests they consider questions of tools (as well as media) unimportant or irrelevant.

Let us pause for a moment to summarize the school model of outlining, as presented in the majority of these textbooks. Leaving aside the occasional moments of doubt (flashes of realism, we might say), the model has these components, in its most common form:

- Note-taking occurs during a research phase, before any outlining.
- The outline is a separate document, distinct from notes and draft.
- The outline is more a product that students should aim to create, than a process they should carry out.
- Outlining occurs during a discrete stage, coming after notetaking, and before drafting.

- Outlining involves organizing one's thoughts "logically."
- Very little writing is involved in outlining—mostly pushing groups of headings into parallel form.
- The outline offers a definitive hierarchical analysis of the topic, with levels indicated by formats and labels. Getting the labels and indentations right is extremely important.
- The outline may need to be revised, but not too often, because any change involves so much recopying.
- The draft must be based tightly on the outline.
- Any new ideas that occur while writing should be inserted in the draft, not the original outline.
- If the structure gets badly skewed during writing, the writer should make a separate, new outline to analyze the structure, with a view to modifying the draft.
- The medium in which the writer creates an outline has no effect on the activities involved, and therefore no impact on the end result; media are function-neutral.

Clearly, among the 75 textbooks we have encountered some disagreements, doubts, and shadings of gray, but on the last point, we find almost total agreement. Not that anyone says, directly, that media make no difference. Rather, no one acknowledges that the model itself is heavily influenced by the expectation that writers will be using paper and ink. We are interested, then, to see to what extent the advent of a dramatically different medium—word processing on the computer—affects the thinking of these textbook authors.

WORD PROCESSING ARRIVES, TRAILED BY OUTLINING SOFTWARE

We might call the period before the 1990s, at least in these textbooks, the age of media innocence. Given their treatment of the typewriter as a tool, we can't be too surprised at how long it took some authors to come to terms with word processing.

The history of word processing begins with the electric typewriter (Price & Urban, 1984). In 1964 IBM brought out the first reusable storage medium for a typewriter—magnetic tape—on their MTST (Magnetic Tape Selectric Typewriter). In 1969 IBM introduced MagCards—magnetic cards that were slipped in a box beside the typewriter. The operator typed on paper and the keystrokes were picked up on the card; the next time the operator wanted to send the same letter, the card could be used to recall (and retype) the text automatically. In 1972 Lexitron and

Linolex added video displays, so users could edit text before committing it to paper—avoiding endless retyping. And in 1973 Vydec added floppy diskettes, which could store the electronic version of every document, for reuse. For the next 10 years, companies selling standalone, "dedicated" word processor machines did a great business. But as the personal computer emerged, with the Apple II in 1978, the IBM PC in 1981, followed quickly by many imitators and the Apple Macintosh in 1984, people realized they could do more than just word processing with a machine costing much less. Unable to adapt, companies like Wang plummeted to bankruptcy. From early computer programs like WordStar, XyWrite, AppleWrite, and MacWrite, the market moved to word processing modules in "integrated packages" such as AppleWorks, Microsoft Works, and ClarisWorks (all stemming from the same original), and then stand-alone applications like Word or Word Perfect within "office suites" (not as tightly integrated as the beginner-level Works packages, but still able to exchange data with a spreadsheet, database, and slide-making program). Beginning in 1985, with Aldus PageMaker, Apple's LaserWriter printer, and Adobe's page-description language PostScript, the desktop publishing trend swept through publishing, along with cold type, electronic graphics, networking, and electronic mail. In response, vendors expanded the capabilities of word-processing products like Word so that they have links to email packages, include a little drawing program, format better than the early desktop publishing programs, and dominate the office market. By the late 1990s, Word has become the lingua franca of business documents.

Unlike paper and pen, the computer is itself a very complex medium, composed of many materials such as electricity, copper, rubber, paint, ink, paper, plastic, silicon, and glass. But what makes any medium usable is the interface of its tools—the aspects we can actually manipulate, directly or indirectly. As users, we might then consider the computer medium to be the electrons inside the computer, the phosphor dots on the screen, the inked paper coming out of its printer. In order to manipulate a medium, we use tools, and with the computer those are hard or soft—the physical hardware, such as the keyboard, mouse, screen, modem, and printer, and then the software, including at a minimum the operating system, and applications such as word-processing packages. When a society regularly works with a certain combination of media and a set of tools, you have a communications technology. In these terms, the textbook authors declined for a long time to say in print that the choice of media and tools could make a difference to the quality of thinking and writing.

Only in the 1990s, some 20 years after word-processing technology began to reach the general public, do the textbook authors acknowledge that some of their readers are using word processing software. And even then, some authors reveal an extremely narrow, and often out-of-date understanding of the electronic medium and word-processing tools. Lester (1990), for instance, talks of dedicated word processing computers five years after those manufacturers had been driven out of business by the surge of personal computers. He seems to think that all word processing software has the commands he remembers from one of those old machines: he has, unfortunately, extrapolated from too narrow experience.

> Your notes can then be moved around easily within the one document by BLOCK moves, which will also help you transfer them quickly into your TEXT document.....Write each note as a separate temporary file so that each can be moved later into the appropriate section of your TEXT file by a COPY or READ command. (p. 106)

Even as late as 1994 Hacker talks as if students were using dedicated word processing machines (p. 60). Bell (1995) includes the antique and rarely used WordStar in his list of "word-processing systems," just as if the year were 1983, and WordStar were a combination of hardware and software, not just an application. Gaffes like these suggest that some of these authors have not taken the time to study the computer as a medium, and word processing as a tool, or that they consider the choice of medium and tools irrelevant to the main purpose of their textbooks.

And what about outlining software? During the 1990s, some textbook authors begin to mention outlining software, as a feature of or alternative to word processing software (Alred et al., 1992, p. 116; Bell, 1995, pp. 88, 90; Brockmann, 1990, p. 24; Hacker, 1994, p. 60; Johnson, 1992, pp. 142-3; Oliu, Brusaw, & Alred, 1995, p. 26.). Johnson (1992) envisions the student taking notes in one file, keeping that open on screen, and creating an outline in another file, then keeping that open while drafting the document in yet another window (pp. 142, 159). Brockmann (1990) recognizes the usefulness of the outliner for large-scale movement of text during revision (p. 24), but Alred and colleagues (1992) argue that the outlining software is so crude it can only be used to analyze the logic of an existing draft, not for "creating logic out of chaotic bits and pieces of information" (p. 116). Of course, Alred and colleagues (1992) quote an article from 1987 as proof that outlining software is "still in its infancy" (p. 116), although by 1992 outlining software was at least eight years old—mature, in terms of software.

Most of these authors simply acknowledge the existence of outlining software, usually as a subset of word processing software, and fail to explore the radical impact of these tools on writing itself, and outlining in particular. Even after the advent of typing and word processing, authors diplomatically discuss outlining as if it were all done with pen on paper, and even with word processing available to most students in college, the authors tend to refer to it as an alternative, or extra option, not a routine tool.

Why the long silence, followed by half-hearted, incomplete, and even inaccurate information? Perhaps some of the authors ignored the emerging technology out of a feeling that many of their colleagues were experiencing—media resentment. The composition folks do, after all, live within English departments, as do many of the technical communications authors. During the 1970s and 1980s, the humanities area as a whole feared the invasion of the computer, and many instructors put off learning anything more than the minimum about word processing software, carping at the personal computer as a glorified typewriter (Kaplan & Moulthrop, 1993; Landow, 1992; Lanham, 1989; Slatin, 1990; Tuman, 1992). In 1985 Daiute said, "Many humanists believe that interacting with machines stifles creativity" (p. 13), and she acknowledges this general anxiety:

> Computers are often portrayed as controlling, dehumanizing, and alienating entities....One controlling computer feature that many people resent is its demand for precision....People also fear that as we program computers to do more and more for us, they will make humans superfluous, and that those uniquely human virtues of unpredictability, creativity, and soul will no longer have value in a machine-dominated society. (p. 7)

Some composition, literature, and rhetoric theorists consider word processing a matter of prettying up the text. Like Halio (1990), who argues that the graphic user interface of the Macintosh somehow led students to write less disciplined papers, Tuman (1992) sees the biggest threat from word processing coming from its graphic options, which he sees undermining the students' effort at critical inquiry in an essay. He believes that graphic design cannot possibly reflect critical thinking or a complex personal vision, bringing together a series of thoughts in a single, coherent document. Of course, Tuman here dismisses the distinguished work of many graphic designers, and the emerging field of document design, so well articulated in Schriver (1997). He seems to think that if there is no printed text, there is no unity. "Indeed, with electronic conversations and different forms of online documentation and electronic presentations, there is no printed form, no document, no unified text" (p.4). We should note that online documentation presents a coherent document, whether one looks at the table of contents, or moves through a section using a Next button. Also, the design of hypertexts, as well as the design of onscreen page layouts, involves a great deal of critical thought, in part because they take users beyond the traditional layout of a dozen or so typed pages, paperclipped together as a report.

Other composition and literature theorists have dismissed word processing as relatively unimportant, compared to other software that seems so much more demonstrably an electronic publishing medium, producing a web of documents with structures and sequencing that cannot easily be captured on paper—hypertext authoring tools, electronic conferencing software, networks, and electronic mail (Barton, 1994; Hawisher, 1991, p. 47; Tuman, 1992, p. 4). Ulmer (1989) laments the decline of the novel and the essay: "The two principal forms of high literacy, invented to exploit fully the specific virtues of the print apparatus...are disintegrating in the culture of electronics, creating a reservoir of simple forms available for new combinations reflecting the capabilities of the new apparatus" (p. 45). Although the computer can be thought of as a mechanical apparatus, it constitutes a new medium, and all of these applications are tools for shaping the medium for communication. Intrigued by the wonderful tools that produce materials that go way beyond paper, many scholars have focused on hypertext authoring packages and the documents created with them. Some forms of hypertext have been staked out as intellectually exciting, because they seem to embody the theories of Barthes and Derrida. (Barthes, 1974, 1982, 1986, particularly pp. 57-62; Derrida, 1973, 1981, 1986; Landow, 1992; Moulthrop, 1989, pp. 20-21). Perhaps our textbook authors, working with and writing for so many people who dismissed word processing as unimportant, decided to downplay the impact of the computer medium and the outlining tool, in a gesture of solidarity.

When an author leaves out a topic, or treats it casually, we cannot always pinpoint the reason for the omission. But omissions themselves are significant—their silence speaks. In this case, the textbook authors evidently did not believe that the choice of medium and tools would have any significant impact on the quality of the thinking, writing, and discussion in the classes using their books.

I disagree, and I would like to take a moment to review some theorists' thinking about the impact of the computer and word processing, and then to explore what else electronic outlining offers—functions regularly ignored or treated casually in these textbooks. Having considered this functionality, we can return to the question of why it has been overlooked.

The computer as a medium offers several advantages over pen and paper. The keyboard helps the user catch up to the speed of thoughts, as it did on the typewriter. The screen and the printer offer far more expressive layout and design, so the user can employ all the techniques of book design such as font, color, and layout to articulate the hierarchical relationships between elements, emphasize the significant, and lead the eye through the argument, in pursuit of the meaning. As Johnson (1997) says, "It's clear that the graphic interface played a crucial role in creating today's colossal market for word-processing applications, a market drawn not only to the functionality of the products but also to their look-and-feel." (p. 142). At the core of the medium are the electrons playing inside the central processing unit, setting switches inside the random-access memory, lighting phosphor dots on the screen, or signaling dot patterns to a printer. Electrons, pixels, and dots all seem quite insubstantial compared to a pen in hand, and a piece of paper.

As Bolter (1991) says, "In the electronic medium several layers of sophisticated technology must intervene between the writer or reader and the coded text" (p. 43). In the same way, Johnson-Eilola (1994) reflects that a hypertext, "because it is electronic, is never completely physically 'there,' never able to be completely located in physical space because it is simultaneously located in the phosphor images on the computer screen; magnetic configurations of volatile silicon computer memory; more permanent floppy, hard, or optical disk storage; and sometimes electrical impulses in phone lines" (pp. 208-9). Of course, such virtuality is true of any electronic document, whether it is a spreadsheet, drawing, or outline.

Thanks to electrons, too, the activity of data entry is separated from the activity of display and both are separated from printout, so when one keyboards a sentence, one is not stuck with ink on paper; the letters appearing on the screen are "just" electronic, and one can change them quickly. Because input is separated from output, any document (text, mathematical formulas, art) can be revised quickly (Price & Korman, 1993, pp. xvii-xviii).

As a result, all electronic data—not just text—seems extraordinarily fluid, when compared to handwritten letters, typed notes, or photocopied materials. (Balestri, 1988; Baudrillard, 1983, p. 115; Bolter, 1991, p. 21; Costanzo, 1994, pp. 11-12; Heim, 1987, 1993; Landow & Delany, 1993, pp. 8-12; Tuman, 1992, p. 57). In fact, the document is freed from our unconscious association with paper; in effect, we no longer think of the document as "a paper." We can now conceive of the document as a single intellectual communication, moving through a number of media environments, from our screen to the paper in the printer, to another person's screen, a thousand miles away, and, perhaps, to the film printer at a production house, then to book or journal pages, photocopies, and finally, archives on the World Wide Web.

Another unique capability of the computer is its responsiveness. The user moves the mouse, then clicks a hot spot on the screen, and it changes color, momentarily, then switches the information displayed on the screen. Daiute (1985) says that some people use the computer "as a tool for writing. This means not only using the computer in much the same way as we use pencils and typewriters, but also exploiting its interactiveness" (p. 17). Costanzo (1994) elaborates: "The computer's responsiveness, its ability to perform quickly on command, to check spelling or suggest alternatives, to recast whole paragraphs in different arrangements for a fresh perspective—all contribute to the sense of a collaborative presence when one is writing deep into the night" (p. 16).

With the advent of the word processing tool, we see additional advantages for writers, most notably the ability to make editorial changes quickly without recopying the rest of the text (e.g., Bernhardt, Edwards, & Wojahn, 1989; Card, Moran, & Newell, 1983; Johnson, 1997; Kellogg, 1994). When handwriting, students may see the opportunity for an improvement, but hesitate, because they are just making more work for themselves. Daiute (1985) says, "Each time they decide to make an improvement, they pay the price of incorporating the change into the text—recopying" (p. 116). Comparing word processing to typing, Daiute (1985) points out how hard it is to back up on the typewriter, apply correction tape or fluid, then restrike (or retype the whole page) compared with the ease with which you can use the Delete or Backspace key on the computer keyboard, to glide over the mistake, eliminating it (p. 35).

The ability to change without recopying allows students to draw up lists of concepts, then move them individually or in clusters, making sense out of the topics by organizing them. These lists form the basis for an outline, whether the student ever turns to the outline view or not. The electronic advantage over paper is, again, that the student can move faster to consider new orders, new groupings, without getting a sore hand.

The ability to avoid "time-consuming recopying or retyping" (Daiute, 1985, p. 36) also encourages students to "act more like experienced writers, who revise extensively" (p. 37). The changes possible include cutting, moving, inserting, finding a word and replacing it, copying a passage and using it in another location or another document—and the changes need not be permanent, thanks to the Undo feature. Daiute comments on this aspect of deletions: "One advantage of electronic erasing is that it is not permanent. Text on paper that is crossed out or painted with correction fluid is no longer visible or usable. In contrast, erasing text on the computer is like putting it in a valise—the buffer. The text can be taken out of the valise and reinserted in a new location in the text" (p. 37).

In a document open to continuous change, users lose a sense of closure. One draft blends into the next, without clear distinctions; the document itself is never really finished, and a printout simply indicates its current stage (Kellogg, 1994; Bernhardt and colleagues, 1989; Daiute, 1985; Hawisher, 1987). What Johnson-Eilola (1994) says of hypertext is true of any interactive software, including word processing: "In one sense, hypertext brings to the surface the resistance to closure, the infinite deferral of a single, univocal meaning in the text, concepts that are sometimes difficult to teach with print texts" (p. 211).

Word processing not only encourages change, it encourages reconsideration, comparison, testing of different approaches, each of which appears in well-formed type on the screen, looking like "final copy" even though it is still in the middle of transformation.

One of the most important opportunities we get when word processing is the chance to experiment with different organizations. Daiute (1985) points out that the software allows a writer to try out several different organizations of ideas without retyping. "By experimenting with alternative organizations or paragraphs, a writer might discover a new idea or a new relationship between the ideas already expressed" (p. 38). On a typewriter, the writer might well stop experimenting after one or two retypings, which take a lot of time, and wear out wrist and fingers. Even Kellogg, who does not believe that word processing improves quality, agrees that "Planning and reviewing are qualitatively different when drafting on a word processor. Moreover, a clear quantitative shift in cognitive effort occurs. The writer plans and reviews more intensely on a word processor" (p. 159).

Clean text onscreen and in immediate printouts give writers distance on the text, compared to the personal "feel" of their own handwriting. Bazerman (1994) points out that the text becomes an object to be inspected, in any writing situation. "In this complex interactive process, text emerges. That text itself becomes an element in the process as something to be inspected and used, as a framework for continuing action" (pp. 14-15).

With word processing on screen and instant printouts, the writer can look objectively at the text more often than with handwriting or typing. Costanzo (1994) argues that the distancing effect of the screen and printout decenters writers from their own texts by "altering the text's appearance through various formatting or fonts." Fitschen (1986) says, "Decentering is the process of stepping back from one's own writing in order to see it afresh before revision" (p. 105). And the computer allows one to do that many times, whereas, for most people, the typewriter limits one to two drafts, or at most three.

In exploring one's own text, a writer takes advantage of word processing's functions to move around quickly within a document, jumping, scrolling, or paging from one location to another, searching for a name or phrase; and to display several documents open at once, within close proximity, for comparison and study.

Of course, skimming is more difficult on screen than on paper, in part because the resolution is so much fuzzier. Close editing, too, suffers from the blurs onscreen, when a comma inside an italic phrase gets lost underneath its slanting neighbor, and a typo does not jump "off the page" to our attention. The computer, though, is not just the screen—the printer is another key component, even though programmers call it a peripheral device. So the computer allows writers to get instant printout, at four to eight times the screen resolution, because printed paper is a more precise medium. Unfortunately, most theorists ignore the printer, treating it as some kind of typewriter add-on; they then complain that browsing and editing is tough when using the computer, when what they really mean is, on the screen (see, for instance, Costanzo, 1994, p. 12).

Word processing's formatting options offer the opportunity to go beyond script or block lettering by hand, and beyond the Courier or Elite fonts most typewriters are limited to, so writers learn to take advantage of font, size, leading, kerning, and color, to indicate differences in emphasis, relationship, and completion (Fortune, 1989). Documents are no longer just texts; they are an interweaving of the visual and verbal (Bernhardt, 1986; Hawisher, 1991; Kaplan & Moulthrop, 1990, p. 100, 1993, p. 262; Landow & Delany, 1993, p. 5; Ruskiewicz, 1988). Not entirely approving, Costanzo (1994) asks, "What does it mean when we spend more time attending to the visual texture of our words than to their content?" (p. 15).

Word processing, then, transforms the process. "The truly interesting thing here," says Johnson (1997), "is that using a word processor changes how we write—not just because we're relying on new tools to get the job done, but also because the computer fundamentally transforms the way we conjure up our sentences, the thought process that runs alongside the writing process" (pp. 142-143). In sum, word processing makes it easier for the writer to carry out a whole range of activities that the textbook authors have always tacitly recommended, but which the earlier media and tools made difficult. Word processing allows the writer to:

- Make extensive changes to the draft (without massive recopying or retyping);
- Experiment with style and organization (picking and choosing the most effective out of several alternatives);
- Get more distance on the document so it can be viewed with more objectivity (by removing the personal flavor of handwriting);
- Turn out fast and multiple publications, for one's own review, or sharing with a group;
- Move around quickly within documents, to ensure consistency, and development; and
- Format expressively, for easier viewing, browsing, and understanding.

Authors like Hult and Harris (1987), and theorists such as Moberg (1986) and Schwartz (1985) have also recognized that word processing makes easier and more visible "the recursive nature of writing, an activity that loops back on itself" (Hawisher, 1991, p. 49). Costanzo (1994), for instance, points out that word processing software "supports theories of composition that regard writing as a recursive process of discovery, elaboration, and revision" because the programs encourage writers to "move back and forth among the stages of generating, developing, organizing, editing, and reconceptualizing texts"(p. 17).

In addition, word processing makes visible many ideas that were, in a pen-and-paper world, fairly hard for students to grasp: the virtuality of text, the deferral of closure, the fact that a creator alternates rapidly between being a reader and a writer, the openness of text in process. Many of these ideas have been found "externalized" (Smith, 1994, p. 280) in hypertext (Balestri, 1988; Johnson-Eilola, 1994; Joyce, 1988; Landow, 1992; Landow & Delany, 1993), but any interactive document, including those being created in word processing, can be taken as a case in point, an object to think with, an exhibit on which to base discussion.

When we turn from word processing to its subset, electronic outlining, we find special additional features that highlight the fluid and evolving nature of the document's structure—capabilities such as a dramatic visual display of the structure, the automatic formatting of any item when it lands at a particular level, the ability to promote or demote topics at a click of the mouse, or to move a topic by dragging it to a new location, the ability to show all the headings of a certain level, while hiding intervening text, the automatic placement of correct labels, whenever a topic is invented or moved to a new location, the ability to append notes, and write full text, within the outline itself. As Bolter (1991) remarks, the outliner sets the traditional outline in motion, treating each topic as a movable unit, where a word processor does the same to individual words. The writer is looking at a visual schematization, putting structure in the forefront. (Compare Streitz, Rizk, & Andre on hypertext, 1990).

What all these outlining functions do is allow the writer to analyze and construct many different organizations more easily than with an ordinary word processor, and a lot more easily than with a typewriter, or pen and paper (Waern, 1989, p. 156). Landow and Delany (1993) point out that print tends to fix the text in one form, making it difficult to work with. "No single arrangement of information proves convenient for all who need that information, and since print, like writing, fixes text in a specific physical form, it causes difficulties for all who do not wish to concentrate on the features emphasized by that particular form" (p. 6).

The writer, I would say, is the first one who needs to be able to consider the information from many different perspectives, weighing alternative organizations. Bolter (1991) points out that "The computer makes visible and almost palpable what writers have always known: that the identifying and arranging of topics is itself an act of writing. Outline processing is writing at a different grain, a replication on a higher level of the conventional act of writing by choosing and arranging words. The symbols of this higher writing are simply longer and more complicated 'words,' verbal gestures that may be whole sentences or paragraphs."

Hypertext pioneers talked of the immense value of alternate views of the same material (Carmody, Gross, Nelson, Rice, & van Dam, 1969, pp. 288-300; Engelbart & English, 1988, pp. 81-105; Meyrowitz & van Dam, 1982, p. 405; Nelson, 1967, pp. 193-195). As Coombs, Renear, and DeRose (1987) say, talking of similar functionality offered by the outline within Standard General Markup Language editors: "The author can easily have the outliner display the outline to any desired depth of detail, the lowest level of detail being the full text, or, perhaps, the text with annotations and alternative versions. ... One may also employ editing utilities to move hierarchical components of the document, as displayed in an outline view, and have the overall document structure adjust accordingly" (p. 110).

In effect, by "exploiting the natural hierarchical structure of text," (Coombs et al., 1987, p. 110), electronic outlining allows one to switch the scale at which one views the material, zooming from a very high-level overview down to minutia, while ignoring as much of the rest of the document as one wishes. What Lanham (1993) calls "this transformatory power of scale-change" (p. 45) allows quick analytical comparisons, confirming that, say, the minor details do indeed belong in a larger section, or that the phrasing of the higher topic genuinely reflects its contents, down to the lowest level. The ability to ignore is at least as valuable as the ability to view, when one is trying to adjust one's focus. One saves time, too, (no more scrolling too far and scrolling back), and that encourages further examination of structure. One can also open two related passages, and close all the intervening text, for easy comparison. The document's genre may dictate a certain sequence for the text elements, but that may separate two topics that are related, in one's mind. The outlining software allows the writer to get beyond the relentless flow of word processing text, to look at the related sections, juxtaposed. (Coombs et al., 1987, p. 109). Coombs and colleagues (1987) say this kind of "structure-oriented" editing (p.110) "enables authors to address their documents at a level of abstraction appropriate to their authorial role" (pp. 111-112), minimizing cognitive demands such as recalling the rest of the structure when working on a particular section (compare Britton, Burgess, Martin, McLeod, & Rosen, 1975, and Kellogg, 1988, 1994), and helping authors focus on content. Kellogg (1994) says that in this sense, the outliner acts as a funnel because it hides distracting information, selectively displaying what the writer is working on, at different levels of the structure:

> For instance, to plan the main ideas of a document, without concern for translating or reviewing those ideas, the writer could collapse the outline and display only its superordinate levels, hiding all subordinate ones. The subordinate levels might prevent the writer from giving full attention to the superordinate one. Thus, in the example, outlining programs encourage the writer to concentrate on high-level planning. Alternatively, to focus on translating a specific subordinate idea, the writer could hide all superordinate levels and expand only the subordinate point of interest at the moment. Once this subordinate point is completely translated, it could be selectively displayed for reviewing as well." (pp. 166-167)

During such structure-oriented editing, the user alternates between being reader and writer (Ward, 1991), trying in both roles to discern a recognizable order, whether it is the conventional structure of a set genre (Beaugrande & Dressler, 1981; Mandler, 1984; van Dijk & Kintsch, 1983, pp. 55-59) or an unconventional, new, and personal structure. As readers, users "understand and learn most easily from texts with well-defined structures that clearly signal shifts between parts," according to Charney (1994, p. 207). She could have been talking about viewing a document in an electronic outline. Considering and reconsidering structure, in whatever ways one wants, also deepens one's understanding of the relationships involved, improving the depth and sophistication of one's thought. Charney, summarizing work by Lodewijks (1982), says that readers who get to regulate their own searches through material by using a structural overview end up with "better recall and better recognition of relations and inferences among the concepts than any of the teacher-provided sequences" (p. 252). Naturally, when the "reader" encounters confusing sequences, the "writer" steps in to clarify, if possible, acting to suture together the chunks, as Johnson-Eilola (1994) suggests writer-readers do when jumping from one hypertext node to another (p. 212), closing what Harpold (1991) calls "the gap in language by the subject's assumption of the place of the gap," binding up the "body of the text" (pp. 177, 176).

In addition to reorganizing the outline, one can write within its framework. Starting with the headings, one can add paragraphs of explanation, exposition, argument, example, or citation, then hide them from view to look around, and get one's bearings. Such a use of an outline fulfills one of the dreams of the textbook authors, that the outline can serve as a map, keeping the writer on track. Daiute (1985) argues that the outline helps the writer learn and remember the overall structure, reminds the writer to include necessary sections, and keeps them to the point. "While free-writing brings up the unexpected, writing with outlines ensures that the expected is included" (p. 81).

In fact, as we have seen, the electronic outliner, by adding structural editing to regular word processing, allows writers to break loose from the lockstep procession of stages, and, instead, work a little on some notes, then step back and see how that new information affects the overall structure, then, inspired, write a few sentences explaining the new vision, then go back to reading another source. Daiute (1985) points out that "as such a report evolves, disorganized notes, semi-organized outlines, outline sections, and paragraphs of varying degrees of completion appear together" (p. 108). Of course, one's aim is always a thoroughly fleshed out, immaculately reasoned document, but on the way there, one does not go through one stage, and then another—rather, one takes different perspectives as one creates.

Perhaps, instead of envisioning these stages as chronological phases, we might recognize that what the authors are grappling with when they talk of stages are simply different activities we engage in, as we move from raw idea to completed document. Activities do not necessarily have to be done in a particular order; in fact, writers tend to do them over and over, in different sequences, depending on what seems most important at the time. Seen as a complex set of interlocking activities, creation is not neat. Writing is a wonderfully messy process.

Of course, working back and forth across the structure can occasionally be confusing, just as navigating hyperspace can lead to hypernausea. But in terms of the sense of place, electronic outlining offers more support for the user. Where users often get lost in hyperspace (Johnson-Eilola, 1994, p. 210, for instance), users of an outlining package can quickly climb back out of the depths, to view their position in the overall structure.

Many of the virtues our theorists have discovered in hypertext also reside, in a different hue, in electronic outlining software. Indeed, an electronic outline can be seen as one view of a menu, and hypertext as another view. The parallels suggest that these different kinds of document have a great deal in common: in fact, they may both belong to a larger class.

Both invite users to participate in reading and writing a document interactively. The electronic outline, like a hypertext, or even an ordinary word processing document, allows extensive interaction; one clicks and goes, in a hypertext, folds and unfolds in the outliner, and edits in the word processing view. Each type of interactive document has aspects of the others, but foregrounds a particular set of functionality. In Word, each type of interactivity appears as a different view of the same document. Where one can manipulate a paper book, opening the index, flipping to a page, skimming a chapter, one interacts with these electronic documents, effectively changing the language, structure, and meaning as one goes, while the document itself responds, grows, and transforms itself on command.

Such a mixed role for the user—what Johnson-Eilola (1994) nostalgically calls the writer/reader—goes one step beyond the neat categories most of the textbook authors take for granted. The textbook authors talk as if the student they address is learning to write, and, on that road, must occasionally read, as if the two activities are distinct. Once people acquire electronic tools, the distinction breaks down in a blur of interactivity.

The document becomes the focal point in a conversation, a temporary artifact that mediates the many dialogs that are taking place (between various identities of the writer, between the writer and an objective representation of the writer's collected earlier thoughts (compare Halliday, 1987), between writer and audience, between the writer's documents and the documents of other writers). Caught at any given moment, the document cannot be said to have a distinct, discoverable meaning. It just represents one turn in the conversation (Bakhtin, 1986), or, to be more precise, several turns in several overlapping conversations, none of which come to a conclusion, reach a decision, or prove any particular idea. As Halliday (1978) suggests, the overall conversation, including everyone's documents and talk, can be considered a sprawling text, "not something that has a beginning and an ending. The exchange of meanings is a continuous process" (p. 136).

These textbooks are books, however, and their authors must have felt a deep commitment to the book as a medium, during the years they spent putting their masterpieces together. Now books have a great interface, a lovely cultural history, and a design that's been developed to a high level of sophistication over hundreds of years, offering many conveniences not available with electronic documents. The reader knows just where the document starts and ends; the reader knows how big it is, just by weighing it; the reader can quickly browse by flipping pages, thanks to the high resolution text; a person can read it on the beach, or in bed; the reader can turn down a page for a bookmark; the reader can switch from one book to another faster than one can open a second window on the screen. But for all these wonderful aspects, a book is a book, and although it can be manipulated, it is not electronic, and so it can never be interactive in the way a document is in word processing, hypertext, or outlining software.

The early silence about electronic outlining, and the more recent casual mentions, may simply reflect the medium in which these textbook authors are writing, and its traditions, which, like blinkers on a horse, keep one headed down the road, without looking to either side. Such media innocence, then, is not a mature virtue. It reflects a half-conscious decision to ignore a large part of the conversation in our overlapping communities. As a result, these textbooks give a distorted picture of the process of creation—a paper model.

NOTES

[1] A horrifying example of this approach to commonplace books was du Maine's vast proposal in 1584 for a French royal library organized in 108 bookshelves, each devoted to a particular subject (such as author, dedicatee, or theme) and containing 100 volumes, each of which would be broken into books about different topics, with chapters about subtopics, notebooks on sub-sub topics, and finally, at the lowest level, commonplaces arranged alphabetically "to locate them more easily." This enormous enterprise, disassembling every printed book, memoir, and manuscript collection du Maine could find, then reassembling the individual passages under his gigantic hierarchical outline, would not contain actual books, but instead, quotations arranged in 108 classes, with appropriate subdivisions, as Erasmus had suggested. Fortunately, the king did not fund du Maine's "universal library." (Chartier, 1994, pp. 74-88).

[2] Andrews & Blickle, 1982, p. 90; Baugh, 1993, p. 67; Bell, 1995, p. 78; Crews, 1980, p. 75; Ehrlich & Murphy, 1964, pp. 28, 37; Hacker & Renshaw, 1979, p. 102; Houp et al., 1995, p. 25; Lester, 1990, pp. 118-120; Markel, 1984, p. 83; Myers, 1955, p. 258; Perrin, 1955, p. 5; Pickett & Laster, 1984, p. 425; Rubens, 1992, p. 16; Sandman et al., 1985, p. 65; Santmyers , 1949, p. 24.; Shelton, 1995, p. 47; Sherman, 1955, p. 9; Smart & Lang, 1943, p. 27; Sypherd, 1957, p. 148.

[3] Alred et al., 1992, p. 113; Leggett et al., 1991, p. 359; Mansfield & Bahniuk, 1981, p.268; Markel, 1984, p. 69; Mills & Walter, 1978, p. 68; Wilcox, 1977, p. 84.

[4] Mansfield & Bahniuk, 1981, p. 268; Markel, 1984, p. 69

[5] Alred et al., 1992, p. 111; Andrews & Blickle, 1982, p. 86; Ehrlich & Murphy, 1964, p. 28; Mansfield & Bahniuk, 1981, p. 268; Santmyers, 1949, p. 32; Tuttle & Brown, 1956, p. 163)

[6] Harwell, 1960, p. 123; Weisman, 1962, p. 268

[7] Alred et al., 1992, p. 111; Alvarez, 1980, p. 157; Dietrich & Brooks, 1958, p. 109; Hays, 1965, p. 104; Leggett et al., 1960, p. 201; Marckwardt & Cassidy, 1960, p. 408; Markel, 1984, p. 70; Mills & Walter, 1962, pp. 60-65; Perrin, 1955, p. 674; Pickett & Laster, 1984, p. 118; Santmyers, 1949,. P. 34; Sherman, 1955, pp. 12-13; Smart & Lang, 1943, pp. 22, 26; Trzyna & Batschelet, 1987, p. 98; Weiss, 1982, p. 52; Wellborn et al., 1961, pp.55-56; Wilcox, 1977, p. 84.

[8] Crews, 1980, p. 74; Elsbree & Bracher, 1967, pp. 30, 42-43; Fowler et al., 1992, pp. 39-40; Johnson, 1992, pp. 141-3; Jordan, 1965, p. 110; Leggett et al., 1960, p. 201; Mansfield & Bahniuk, 1981, p. 268; Marckwardt & Cassidy, 1960, pp. 410-1; Mills & Walter, 1962, p. 45; Mills & Walter, 1978, pp. 55-60; Naylor, 1942, pp. 48-9; Pearsall & Cunningham, 1978, p. 272; Perrin, 1955, p. 674; Santmyers, 1949, p. 31; Sherman, 1955, pp. 12-13; Smart & Lang, 1943, p. 26; Thomas, 1949, pp. 132-5; Trzyna & Batschelet, 1987, pp. 98, 103; Weiss, 1982, p. 51; Wellborn, 1961, p. 56; Wicker & Albrecht, 1960, pp. 54-58; Wilcox, 1977, p. 87.

[9] Alred et al., 1992, p. 111; Mansfield & Bahniuk 1981, p. 268; Sandman et al., 1985, p. 63; Tuttle & Brown, 1956, p. 162; Weisman, 1962, p. 261

[10] Alred et al., 1992, pp. 111, 115; Alvarez, 1980, p. 176; Mills & Walter, 1978, pp. 55-65; Trzyna & Batschelet, 1987, p. 98; Weisman, 1962, pp. 261, 268; Weiss, 1982, p. 52; Wilcox, 1977, p. 84.

[11] Alred et al., 1992, pp. 113-114; Weisman, 1962, p. 268.

[12] Alred et al., 1992, p. 114; Alvarez, 1980, p. 176.

[13] Hacker & Renshaw 1979, p. 108; Weiss, 1982, p. 52

[14] Alvarez, 1980, p. 176; Leggett et al., 1960, p. 202; Smart,1943, p. 26; Weiss 1982 52

[15] Harwell, 1960, p. 28; Leggett et al., 1991, p. 359; Lester, 1990, p. 120; Thomas, 1949, p. 131; Ward, 1968, p. 68; Wicker & Albrecht, 1960, p. 56

[16] Alred et al., 1992, p. 114; Alvarez, 1980, p. 176; Brusaw et al., 1993, p. 488; Sherman, 1955, p. 13; Weisman, 1962, p. 261

[17] Alvarez, 1980, p. 176; Smart & Lang, 1943, p. 26

[18] Myers, 1955, p. 259

[19] Harwell, 1960, p. 123; Perrin, 1955, p. 674.

[20] Alred et al., 1992, p. 113, Alvarez, 1980, p. 157; Andrews & Blickle, 1982, pp. 86-88; Brusaw et al., 1993, p. 488; Ehrlich & Murphy, 1964, p. 48; Hacker & Renshaw, 1979, p. 108; Hacker, 1994, p. 27; Leggett et al., 1991, p. 359; Mansfield & Bahniuk, 1981, p. 268; Markel, 1984, p. 70; Perrin, 1955, p. 13; Rubens, 1992, p. 19; Sandman et al., 1985, p. 63; Santmyers, 1949, p. 32; Trzyna & Batschelet, 1987, p. 102; Tuttle & Brown, 1956, p. 163; Weisman, 1962, pp. 261-8; Weiss, 1982, p. 52; Wilcox, 1977, p. 84.

5
Why Outline?

W hy bother outlining? It's a question millions of students have asked and, as we develop a theory of outlining, we need to ponder the answers we offer them. The answers provided by textbooks suggest what the authors hoped young writers would get out of the experience of outlining—benefits that round out the authors' model of the outline, reflecting the way it grows out of their cultural situation. Working in fields such as technical writing, engineering writing, and composition, these authors often had to defend their work as serious, intellectual, and almost scientific, within university settings; as useful and practical, within a late-capitalist economy; and as expressive, satisfying, and even meaningful, in the context of writing as a whole, including more creative work. As a result, we see them attributing logic, practicality, and art to the paper outline.

When we explored electronic outlining, we found a number of potential benefits compared to paper outlines, such as greater openness, opportunity for thought, and collaboration. The electronic process allows continual revision of the structure, as the writers keep reconsidering the information, and moving toward what becomes ultimately a more accurate, more expressive structure, on behalf of the audience. Structure is always open to new insight and new facts. Also, the activities encouraged by the software resemble those of ordinary thought, made easier by the functionality of the outliner. Improving the structure yields greater understanding for the writers. Nothing has to be left out, or included, because of a rigid separation of tasks: The writer can cycle back and forth from research to structure to draft, because outlining is simply one view of the emerging document. And, focusing on the outline as a tool for achieving mutual understanding, a team of writers can use the software to collaborate in ways they could never manage before. ·

On the other hand, when the textbook authors turn from straightforward description and prescription to persuasion, they seem to recognize that some of their readers may feel a deep antipathy to outlining. To counter that resistance, the authors adopt three main positions when arguing in favor of outlining: 1) they claim that outlining is a logical activity, 2) they claim that outlining will save time and money, and 3) they hint, metaphorically, that outlining will help the student shape and grow a unified, organic whole, which will solidify into some form such as a map or blueprint, to serve as a useful guide when the student actually writes the draft.

The effort to articulate the benefits of outlining adds depth and shading to the rather stark picture the textbook authors present in their passages of analysis and instruction. We can see more of what they thought intellectually beneficial, practically useful, and psychologically satisfying about the activities involved. Considering this aspect of the textbooks also lets us glimpse a human side of the authors, as teachers and fellow writers.

EMPHASIZING THE LOGIC OF AN OUTLINE

In the textbooks, outlining is often presented as a way to avoid a set of common problems found in student writing. A typical student paper is seen as an unbalanced, poorly shaped jumble of "casual or misfitting bits" (Marckwardt & Cassidy, 1960, p. 8), an incoherent assemblage lacking unity, proportion, emphasis, sequence of thought, focus, and coordination (Wicker & Albrecht, 1960, p. 51), an arrangement of parts without logical sequence, some overdeveloped, some skimped (Wilcox, 1977, p. 83). The fundamental problem underlying all of these organizational errors is poor thinking, according to the vast majority of these authors. Dietrich and Brooks (1958) buttonhole their reader: "Why take the time and effort? For the following reasons: Outlining is the only satisfactory way of getting your ideas down in a logical, meaningful sequence. Outlining forces straight thinking; if the ideas don't fit, the outline will show it" (pp. 109-110).

Alred and colleagues (1992) agree; the outline "exposes errors in your logic" (p. 111). The same authors (Brusaw et al., 1993) add: "Errors in logic are much easier to detect in an outline than in a draft" (p. 485).

So students need to make outlines to wrestle their ideas into a logical order. Logic, in fact, is the Ramus-like ghost behind almost all these textbooks; logic appears as the guiding light, the justification, and the very theme of the discussion of outlines. To outline, many authors imply, all you have to do is analyze the material logically.[1] But what logic are we talking about, exactly?

Evidently, it is logical to insist that all essential points be included, and all irrelevant points excluded (Smart & Lang,, 1943, pp. 19-20). But how does logic pick these essential points in the first place?

Just how a writer discovers the nature of the subject is, well, perhaps a little illogical. One just gets some ideas. Perhaps one researches a subject, perhaps one noodles around on a pad, but eventually one comes up with some major topics. Then, according to these textbook authors, one applies logic, to develop the outline. Logic, to them, involves three main processes: division or subordination, grouping or coordination, and sequencing in a familiar order.

Division

The majority of these authors see logical division as one of the most important activities in creating an outline.[2] Given a handful of important topics, the writer must divide each topic into at least two subtopics. Why? "The reason for this procedure is sheer logic," say Leggett and colleagues (1960): "Each breakdown of the outline is a division of a foregoing bigger point, and you cannot logically divide something into just one part. A single subheading reflects poor organization and should be incorporated into the heading of which it is **logically** a part" (p. 201).

Certainly, that is one way of creating a structure, but many of these authors have gotten carried away with their own assumptions. We could just as easily say an outline represents an accumulation of examples from which we can emerge with a summary heading by induction. We could note also that many outlines simply represent a template that a profession has settled on, because its pattern forces authors to answer many of the questions readers ask. So reality is not what is forcing textbook authors to think this way. To consider why the authors so often emphasize the logic of division, we may need to consider their social and historical context.

Just as technical writing textbooks during the first 40 years of the century urged budding engineers to adopt professional language, and talk with the same broad learning as a lawyer or doctor, to demonstrate that engineers, too, were professionals (Hagge, 1995), so some of the composition and technical writing authors for the second half of the 20th century seem to dress themselves in the language of other, more "logical" disciplines such as mathematics, biology, and philosophy—perhaps to acquire some of their academic and professional dignity.

Hagge (1995) investigated the first 20 American technical writing textbooks published, all of which he positions within the field of engineering education. These books appeared between 1908 and 1938, the height of a period during which "modern technical communication was institutionalized" (p. 444). Explaining his method, Hagge cites Greene (1957/58) "The primary function of the intellectual historian is to delineate the presuppositions of thought in given historical epochs and to explain the changes which those presuppositions undergo from epoch to epoch....[One does this through] close examination of source materials for underlying premises, with special attention to the connotations of words and to the recurrence of stock phrases" (Hagge, 1995, p. 447, quoting Greene, 1957-1958, pp. 59, 73).

Applying this kind of close historical reading to these early texts, Hagge concludes that the authors recommended conventional organizations and a formal style to meet the needs and expectations of readers (pp. 450-456)—and in order "to project linguistically a dignified, status-maintaining image of their profession, which is often compared with earlier and more traditional American professions" (p. 474). "Thus learning to write proficiently, particularly in business, scientific, and technical settings is largely a matter of enculturation into the linguistic conventions of a particular disciplinary discourse community. It relies much less on the free play of individual creativity while composing and revising, as claimed especially in early process research (e.g. Emig, 1977; Perl, 1979, 1980; Pianko, 1979; Sommers, 1980), than it does on adapting preestablished conventions to particular rhetorical situations" (Hagge, 1987, p. 441).

To judge from the textbooks in technical writing from the 1940s to the present, the battle that engineers had to wage for respect as a profession was won during World War II. After the wartime films, radio broadcasts, and newspaper articles had advertised manufacturing and technology as part of our victories, scientists and engineers were seen as almost as heroic, and certainly better paid, than soldiers. Few technical writing books after 1945 make the arguments Hagge found for professional dignity, custom, and conventional organization. The focus becomes more practical, more focussed on communicating to get a job done. The audience widens to include non-engineers, even English majors seeking jobs as technical writers. This significant broadening of the audience has led the authors to see technical communication at the core of a new field, living in uneasy alliance with engineering and English departments. At the same time, composition emerged as an unacknowledged ghetto within English departments, and then in the 1960s began to forge its own identity, through research and theory. In uncertain discourse situations, any difficult or unpleasant aspect of the writing process begins to require some justification. The post-World-War-II authors of technical communication textbooks seem to feel a need to justify the process of outlining by making it seem almost as rigorous (and respectable) as engineering itself had become. Authors of composition and rhetoric books began to take a similar approach—claiming for outlines the virtues of mathematics, architectural engineering, and modern business, rather than the blessings of a cultural tradition dating back to classical Greece and Rome, like the canon McDonald (1929) had praised: "Such a common background among educated men made for ease of expression and for a sympathy that permitted a valuable basis for cooperation" (p. 161).

Hagge (1995) stresses that writing is "a highly complex sociolinguistic act dependent on a mutual knowledge of a shared context, including explicitly articulated and socially reinforced discourse conventions" (p. 441). Writing one of these textbooks puts an author in just such a complicated situation, responding to the needs and complaints of previous and anticipated students, keeping colleagues' opinions in mind, and trying to understand, articulate, and justify all the activities being recommended—including outlining. As Hagge says, "Such a theoretical foundation argues strongly for investigations of writing that focus mainly on written texts, the situational context in which they are embedded, the development of the discourse conventions of which they are composed, and the metacommentary that often justifies the institutionalization of these conventions" (p. 442).

Let's look more closely, then, at the way these textbook authors justify division as the primary logical tool to use when outlining. In a magnificent attempt to give mathematical underpinnings to what they call "the logic of outlines" Mills and Walter (1962) argue that dividing topics into subtopics is the main activity you need to carry out when creating an outline. Watch the assumptions swell and grow mathematical:

> The fundamental principle of outlining is division. The subject to be outlined is divided into major parts (Roman-numeral divisions); these major parts are divided into subparts (capital-letter divisions); these subpart divisions are divided into sub-subparts (Arabic numeral divisions); and so the whole is divided into smaller and smaller units to whatever degree seems desirable.

> Since outlining is a method of dividing, it naturally conforms, in a certain degree, to the principles of arithmetic. Let X equal the entire subject to be divided, or outlined. Then $X = I + II + III \dots n$. In turn, $I = A + B + C \dots n$ and $A = 1 + 2 + 3 + \dots n$. And so forth. Please understand that this is more than an analogy. It is a principle which not only can be but should be applied to every outline you write, to test its logical soundness. (p. 45)

Following this line, several writers use a mathematical style to justify the rule. Wicker and Albrecht (1960) say, "The result of a division obviously cannot be one" (p. 58). Elsbree and Bracher (1967) say, "The argument is that dividing something produces at least two parts if it is a genuine division" (p. 143). Weiss (1982) says "Nothing can be partitioned or subdivided into only one part!"(p. 51).

However, when a number is divided by itself, we get a quotient of one, a valid result, so the mathematical analogy only carries us so far. In real life, we may have a topic with a single subtopic when, for instance, we are describing all the panels on a box, with their functions, and the final panel has only one button on it. But sixteen years later, Mills and Walter (1978) returned to the argument with such an expanded mathematical discussion that we sense they are using the mathematical overtones to pull outlining out of the context of English, and give it some of the sensible, quantitative elegance of science and engineering.

Similarly, Jordan (1965) associates division and grouping with the classification process in biology: "A basic problem in this process of classification is how many main pigeonholes to set up. As a certain biology professor used to tell his classes, 'All the world is divided into splitters and lumpers.' He was talking about scientists who classify living organisms; but makers of outlines must also decide whether to set up a new category or consider an idea a subspecies of an existent group. To split, or lump?" (p. 110).

Many authors discuss subordination as an act of reasoning similar to thinking in philosophy or psychology, but beg the question of what makes one person's subordination logical, and another's illogical. Wilcox (1977) praises an outline because it can tell writers at a glance whether "the subpoints are logically related to the points to which they are subordinate" (p. 83). Perhaps he just means that if the writers can reason a little, they can figure out what the relationships are. Damerst (1982) starts off claiming logic is easy to see, but then, at the end redefines logic in psychological terms, as "the way our minds work" (p. 59), which seems distinctly odd, in the century of Freud and Hitler.

Why divide? Just because logic tells us to, evidently. And, despite the borrowed glamour, the authors' use of the term *logic* seems, at best, to refer to common ways of thinking, not the methods of formal logic in mathematics, computer science, or philosophy. In this borrowed context, the stress on division appears almost axiomatic, a first principle that cannot be questioned, or demonstrated.

Grouping

"Logic" also dictates grouping related subjects together. "All material which is logically a part of one topic should be assembled under one heading," say Smart and Lang (1943, p. 22). Again, faced with practical choices, a writer may wonder exactly what kind of logic to use, here. Pickett and Laster (1984) praise outlines for "grouping items in an orderly, systematic arrangement" (p. 118). Markel (1984) stresses coordination. "Coordination is the process of identifying two or more items as roughly equivalent in importance" (p. 72). So logical grouping seems to involve putting together related items of equal importance in some system. Again, when looked at more closely, logic in this sense boils down to little more than sorting topics by category.

Sequencing

"Logic," too, supposedly dictates the sequence of groups of topics, or subtopics. "The list of topics, logically grouped and arranged, now forms a simple working outline," say Smart and Lang (1943, p. 22). But what is a logical arrangement? Other authors emphasize that the sequence should be "logical" (Alvarez, 1980, p. 157; Dietrich & Brooks, 1958, p. 109; Leggett et al., 1960, p. 201; Marckwardt & Cassidy, 1960, p. 408; Markel, 1984, p. 70; Santmyers, 1949, p. 34; Sherman, 1955, p. 12; Weiss, 1982, p. 52; Wellborn et al., 1961, p. 55; Wilcox, 1977, p. 86). For instance, Hays (1965) says, "Outlines usually follow a logical order or a combination of logical orders" (p. 104). It's good to see that one can have a combination of these logical orders, but what are they? Generally, they turn out to be familiar patterns such as chronological order, cause and effect, problem and solution, and so on. Having asserted the need for logical sequences, Wilcox (1977) backs off when he actually describes these sequences, settling for the term "patterns." "Our review above of patterns and their uses quite clearly implies that a message may possess not just one pattern but many, and the longer the message the greater number of patterns" (p. 81). These ways of thinking about a topic can hardly be called logical unless we define that as "following common habits of thinking"; they are simply popular ways of organizing data, and, to that extent, reveal reasoning. But is that enough to justify calling these schemas "logic?"

Discipline Envy

This concern with logic as an activity and as a cloak of respectability may derive in part from discipline envy. In the 1940s and 1950s, I gather from these texts, composition envied the logic of classical philosophy, technical communication envied composition, and both fields envied the precision of mathematics, and the classification schemes of science. Discipline envy may be taken as a sign of a developing, or uncertain discipline, compared to the self-referentiality with which a mature profession defines its purposes. Sinfield (1992) for instance says that "The tendency of a profession is to become self-referential" (p. 287). Of course, Sinfield imagines that a profession only once establishes its own criteria about what members are supposed to be doing, within the profession; but any mature profession continues to debate its purpose, meaning, and methods, incorporating new content, new approaches, and new explanations of significance, always articulating itself in contrast to other disciplines. For instance, restless with the constraints imposed by earlier definitions of the field, the new historicists such as Greenblatt (Greenblatt, 1980, 1988a, 1988b; Greenblatt & Gunn, 1992; Thomas, 1991) have urged that the boundaries of literary studies be expanded, to include other disciplines, such as history—or, as Fish (1995) would say, disapprovingly, to leave literary work and become some other discipline altogether.

However, our textbook authors are hardly arguing that composition or technical writing has become too tightly defined, too limiting as a discipline, and needs to be opened up, to bring in fresh air from other disciplines. And the authors are certainly not arguing for the end of disciplines, for the sake of some undefined, but unified knowledge, without petty border disputes (Agger, 1992; Messer-Davidow, Shumway, & Sylvan 1993). They are not, for instance, following the banner of Brantlinger (1990) "to overcome the disabling fragmentation of knowledge within the disciplinary structure of the university" (p. 16). Or at least, if they are engaged in that struggle, they do not say so. The impulse to credit outlining with more logic than it deserves, in my opinion, is more unconscious than these guerilla movements, less grounded in theory, springing more likely from personal attempts to articulate the real reasons the authors want students to learn to outline. In effect, the appeal to logic betrays some of the innocence of a developing field.

Despite their increasing reliance on the flourishing research on how people learn, how people actually write, and how people learn to write, these textbook authors are still more like the people North (1987) called practitioners, in his controversial survey of composition studies. Practitioners, in his terms, accumulate lore, which is concerned mostly "with what has worked, is working, or might work in teaching, doing, or learning writing" (p. 23). Clearly, this argument from logic has worked for many teachers over the years, even though it is not explicitly tied to experimental research, or to some overarching theory. Practitioners don't care much whether they are borrowing ideas or respectability from another field, as long as it helps students succeed at writing.

Another force driving these authors to emphasize the reasoning involved in outlining may be the ambiguous "service" mission handed to them by other departments within the university. For the last half century, both composition and technical writing instructors have felt intense pressure from their home departments (whether English, Engineering, or some vaguer umbrella, such as Humanities), and from the entire university to train students in writing one particular form, the essay. Through this period, the essay has represented the height of rational arguments (Daiute, 1985, p. 30), associated with progress, the civilizing influence of the university, and the upward mobility supposedly waiting for students when they graduate. In describing composition's attempts to train students to write a formal, argumentative essay as far back as the 1940s, Bilsky and colleagues (1953) say: "It is widely believed that courses in composition should deal with argumentation; and few question that argumentation is related to logic" (p. 210).

The essay, starting with a thesis statement, followed by a series of arguments intended to prove the statement, ends with a conclusion that, after all, the thesis is true. In terms of structure, of course, the essay is just another form that one can outline. Given the mission assigned to composition classes, though, we are not surprised that every composition textbook shows students how to outline an essay, and nothing else. Some technical writing textbooks also act as if the only thing a technical writer will ever write is some variation on an essay. Odd, for an industry in which many genres do not begin with a thesis statement, do not provide evidence for any particular idea (except that the product being described is wonderful), and follow organizational patterns set up by professional societies, industry-wide consortia, marketing honchos, and government agencies, to meet the needs of clients who want an airplane manual, quick reference, tutorial, how-to guide, trouble-shooting diagnostic, or installation guide, not an academic essay. The closest most technical writers come to writing essays is developing reports and proposals, which do revolve around a central idea, and tend to prove that the research should be funded, or renewed, because it has revised our understanding of some important subject in science or engineering. So reports get a heavy emphasis in these textbooks.

Many of the technical writing authors stress the thesis statement, that single most characteristic element of an essay, as a way of organizing information around a central idea. For instance, Thomas (1949) rhapsodizes:"The first part of a sentence outline, and the most important single entry, is the thesis sentence, which states the unifying idea of the composition in one sentence. The thesis is the paper in miniature, a reduction of the whole plan to a single sentence in which every thought to be deveoped is present in germ" (p. 131).

Thomas (1949) admits that this pattern "is not the only sound manner of organization" (p. 140), but other authors don't even blink. Wicker and Albrecht (1960), for instance, argue that your outline should have "a conclusion just as every piece of formal discourse should have" (p. 56). Hartwell (1960) says, "The first step is to set down the purpose of the paper; and work out the thesis. The thesis is a precisely worded statement of the central idea the paper is to convey; it is the magnet that holds the paper together" (p. 28). Similarly, Ward (1968) urges, "As early as possible in the preparation of an outline, a thesis statement should be crystallized. This is a well-rounded expression—in a single sentence—of the key idea of the presentation. It answers the key question that the report set s out to deal with" (p. 68).

Of course, some of the technical communication authors recognize that the essay is not the only organization their students will be called upon to write. For instance, Hays (1965), Schmidt (1983), Weiss (1982), and Young (1989) acknowledge that technical writers may simply be handed a standard order of topics, into which the writer must insert boilerplate taken from other documents, as with some military documentation (Hays, 1965, p. 102). But aside from these books, the vast majority of both composition and technical writing books take bows, both deep and shallow, to the essay, as the product of all this outlining, and the justification for applying these "logical" tools to the material.

What, then, are we to make of all this logic? First, that the process of outlining does, indeed, involve a fair amount of thinking, particularly grouping, partitioning, and sequencing. And, although an outline serves almost any structure well, it probably helps some writers develop their arguments for an essay. However, exaggerating the logicalness of outlines, these authors go beyond the truth (that outlining involves sorting one's ideas in common patterns other folks will recognize). These authors enter the arena of marketing, claiming the aura of much more strenuous disciplines, for whom logic is a matter of formal rules and strict methods. The authors have moved outlining away from the soft area of traditional English studies (the interpretation of poetry, drama, and the novel, say) and towards the hard disciplines of mathematics, philosophy, science, and engineering—without, of course, insisting students apply any of the rigor of those disciplines. Like a manufacturer claiming their cars are solid as a rock, the textbook authors seem to be indulging in wishful thinking.

Also, by focussing so heavily on the genre of the essay, the authors imply that every document one might outline will turn out to be an essay. Of course, many composition courses have been set up to serve the university by training all students in that essential genre of academic life, so the authors of composition texts need to follow their market; but technical communication texts often talk the same way, mentioning "thesis statement" as if it were necessarily the first thing a writer should put in an outline. (What is the thesis statement of a network configuration guide?)

The outline can also help surface the structure of an argument, if necessary. But because the essay is built as a chain of reasoning, the authors find it easy to suggest that the "logic" of the outline helps build the "logic" of the essay. And within the university as a whole, the essay, in the form of journal article, book, proposal, or report, is the most respected genre, so we see that the outline is, again, in excellent company.

The exaggerated claims of logic and the association with the academic essay, then, act as two main persuasive appeals on behalf of outlining. Hyperbole, or exaggeration, has always been a rhetorical tool, taking the ordinary and making it seem jumbo, to express enthusiasm for the subject. However, by describing everyday habits of thought (organizing by chronology or point, say) as if they were the algorithms of mathematical logic, the authors make the resulting order sound like the abstract pattern of a Fibonacci sequence, rather than a simple structure most people can recognize and follow.

Logic, then, is presented as somehow at the core of the thinking process that creates an outline, and an essay is seen as the ideal form to build this way. But glorious as these ideals may be to the textbook authors themselves, these standards of civilization (or totems of the tribe) do not always inspire students, as the authors sometimes acknowledge (Coe, 1981, p. 9; Fowler et al., 1992, p. 35; Hacker & Renshaw, 1979, p. 108; Myers, 1955, p. 257; Rose, 1980, p. 389; Young, 1989, p. 141). In fact, all this talk of reasoning sounds suspiciously like work—possibly extra work, unnecessary, arbitrary, and "just academic" work at that. So the authors turn to other arguments to persuade students to create outlines.

Having rubbed outlines with the gold dust of logic, giving it the glow of other disciplines, and having connected outlines directly to the essay, the monarch of academic genres, the authors seem to have sensed that such arguments may actually appeal more to their colleagues, and themselves, than to students. The conversation is more complex than it seems, involving at least two different audiences for the textbook—other teachers, and, oh yes, students. So now we encounter a set of appeals aimed directly at the students' self-interest, in practical, businesslike terms.

REASSURING STUDENTS THAT AN OUTLINE CAN BE A PRACTICAL TIME-SAVER

Many textbooks include at least one appeal to the student writer as a person at work on a document—making a psychological or practical argument for outlining, distinct from the threnodies about logic. The authors seem to reason from their own experience as practitioners of writing and teaching, in North's (1987) sense, trying to describe the ways that outlining can ameliorate one's own mental state, and improve one's work efficiency. But in these attempts to motivate students, the textbook authors sometimes go further, implying that an outline offers the magical transformations we've heard about in TV commercials (Price, 1978), giving the writers self confidence, saving them time and money, and making life (or at least writing) easier.

Some textbook authors assume that part of what's stopping, or confusing, student writers is nervousness. Perrin (1955) claims outlines remove anxieties: "In fact a good working plan will remove most of your worst worries, for there is nothing more discouraging than to have to pause in the middle of rapid writing to wonder if a certain point really goes there" (p. 15).

Crews (1980) identifies a similar set of emotions attacking the writer of a first draft: reluctance, anxiety, uncertainty, and fear. So the outline plays the role of demon-killer.

> Nothing is more normal than a feeling of reluctance and anxiety during the writing of a first draft. Those first few paragraphs are likely to prove especially troublesome. Since the great enemy of the first draft is uncertainty, however, you will find your work much less awesome if you have on hand ample notes, a fully developed thesis statement, and an outline that looks— at least for now—logical and efficient. These are your safe passes into that scary realm, the Not Yet Written. Knowing (from your thesis statement) that you have a clear and interesting point to make, and knowing (from your outline) that the paragraph you are struggling with now belongs in an order sequence, you can talk back to that little demon who keeps saying, "You're stuck, you're stuck, you're stuck...." (p. 75)

A similar appeal is that making an outline will save the writer time (Hammond & Allen, 1953, p. 58; Hays, 1965, p. 199; Shelton, 1995, p. 41; Ward, 1968, p. 70). Of course, this argument directly contradicts the suspicion of most students that outlining is some form of busywork. Why should they bother? Ehrlich and Murphy (1964) put it this way: "Without an outline to work from, you will waste time in excessive, extensive rewriting" (p. 28). Wilcox (1977) argues directly with students who feel that outlining is a waste of time: "Writers who expect to conserve time by skipping the outlining stage invariably waste time instead" (p. 83).

You can revise structure more quickly in an outline than in a running text, the argument goes. Andrews and Blickle (1992) say, "An organization that appears defective in outline form can be dropped in favor of a more effective plan before the text even begins to emerge. It is enormously time consuming to write out one full composition after another in search of the most efficient scheme of organization. The outline can be reviewed and tested, modified, refined, scrapped, redone; as much time as this takes, it is bound to be less than that required to write a whole report in draft form to represent each different organizational approach" (p. 86).

Alred and colleagues (1992) quote a professional writer to the same effect:"I guess I would say you would ultimately save time by organizing before you get to the detail level. Because it's a lot harder to move chunks of information around in a text when they are already in full paragraphs. Lots of times you've already written transitions between paragraphs. Then, when you move a paragraph to another page, you have a lot more rewriting to do. It's just a lot easier to rearrange things when you're working at the more general level of an outline" (p.120).

Outlining can save writers money, too, if they do it in business and government. Echoing commercials for stock brokers and insurance companies, Harwell (1960) says about outlining that "Writing it may take time but it will prove a sound investment. For each minute we give to careful outlining, we are well repaid when we undertake the actual writing. We are repaid in quantitative measure by saving time; we do not have to rearrange material and rewrite passages. And we are repaid in a qualitative way; our finished paper has a smoothness and compactness it might not have otherwise" (p. 28).

Hays (1965), taking an even more business-oriented view of the situation, calls an outline an insurance policy:

> An outline may be a cheap insurance policy against wasted time, even if the reader does not request an outline. A rough plan for the report is a safe dry run....A customer should change his mind about what he wants in a report before the writer starts writing, not after lithographed copies have been bound. If the writer shows such supervisors an outline before he spends too much time in writing the report, he forestalls some future criticism. The supervisor (or the difficult client) will hesitate to order a complete revision in a report if he approved the original outline. An outline may also force a reader to explain more clearly what he expects. (p.101)

Markel (1984) makes the most practical pitch for the outline as a good investment: "Taking the time to work out a careful outline and write a rough draft is like changing your oil and filter when you're supposed to— it's cheaper in the long run" (p. 67).

The arguments that outlining will save the writer's time and money seem to start from a common but often unstated assumption that a writer will probably have to revise the organization of the material at some time or other, perhaps several times. If that's so, outlining has another appeal: it makes revising structure easier, according to several authors.

These authors argue that doing the restructuring in the outline is easier than doing it in draft. Tuttle and Brown (1956) say, "It is much easier to switch things around in an outline than after they have been written out in full" (p. 163). Wilcox (1977) says an outline can tell the writer, "almost at a glance," whether the plan is sound (p. 83). Shelton (1995) concurs: "If, while looking over an outline, you notice a violation of logic or fact, you can make the change far easier and faster than trying to pick it out of the finished text" (p. 42).

I agree that outlining helps allay fears, saves time and money, and makes restructuring easier, but these statements are not designed just to describe outlining in a neutral way. These are arguments borrowed from late-capitalist culture intended to persuade students it is in their self-interest to act—to get out there and outline.

Evidently, the authors have developed these arguments when responding to students they've had in the past—students just like those who are the intended readers of these books. The first argument responds to students who say they feel nervous and anxious, not knowing what to write. The next two arguments respond to students who say they feel outlining takes too much time—a poor way to invest their energy, and a waste of money, if they are in business. The last denies the students' claim that outlining is just too darn hard. Anyone who's taught or been taught outlining has participated in these exchanges, I imagine, and they echo through these pages, a dialog in which we usually hear the authors more distinctly, though the students are always muttering in the background.

Perhaps it was the strain of these arguments that drove the textbook authors to adopt the tones of Madison Avenue and the terms of the marketplace—efficiency, getting unblocked, saving time and money, and convenience. But the authors do not seem content to leave the matter there. Having portrayed their students as aspiring logicians and productivity-minded entrepreneurs, they seem to realize that fundamentally the students are young writers, who face challenges of artistry, meaning, and expression.

Hence, we also see the textbook authors taking another view of their readers, considering them as writers struggling to shape and create. Perhaps because this view of their audience, the authors express these less tangible benefits through metaphor.

USING METAPHOR TO EXPRESS THE BENEFITS OF OUTLINING

Many textbook authors reach out for metaphor as a way to express the less rational and less practical benefits of outlining, suggesting, for instance, that the process helps writers make a meaningful structure visible, allows writers to keep reorganizing as they struggle to envision the very best structure for their thinking about the material, drawing together a multitude of topics, unifying them in an organic, growing whole.

The metaphors these textbook authors use to describe outlining seem to reflect their own personal experiences as writers organizing their materials, as teachers trying to persuade students that outlining can be beneficial, as colleagues discussing outlines with peers, and as textbook authors reading what other textbooks have to say. In that sense, these metaphors are personally and socially expressive. However, considered as a whole, the metaphors chosen tend to follow several common motifs, and behind those, we can discern a set of ideas that go significantly beyond those dealing with logic and practicality.

Metaphor comes trailing implications, suggesting concepts, hinting at related fields and experiences. Lakoff and Johnson (1980) point out that we "draw inferences, set goals, make commitments, and execute plans, all on the basis of how we structure our experience, consciously and unconsciously, by means of metaphor" (p. 484), because metaphor entails certain ideas. In this section, I explore some of the ideas entailed by the metaphors that the textbook authors use when encouraging students to outline.

Several textbook authors compare the outline to an artist's first sketch, in which the charcoal lines block out the major elements on the canvas, without fixing anything too permanently in place. Emphasizing the roughness and unfinished nature of the outline, as well as its role in surrounding the material, defining the borders, and placing the major elements in the composition as a whole, these authors return to the etymology of the word *outline*. One of the leading shapers of the freshman composition program at Harvard, Martin (1957), for instance, takes an artist's view: "As the underlying metaphor implies, an outline describes the circumference of an essay and of each of its various parts....An outline developed from such a series of assertions is immediately useful to the writer; with it before him, he can work swiftly and efficiently, explaining and expanding each assertion, 'filling in' the outline with the corroborative and illustrative data he has accumulated by research and reflection" (pp. 138-139).

The "sketch" metaphor helps authors reassure students that the outline itself is just a part of the process. Fowler and colleagues (1992) say, "You should view any outline you make as a tentative sketch, not as a fixed paint-by-numbers diagram" (p. 35). Here, the outline acquires overtones of art, going beyond any merely mechanical craft.

By comparing the outline to an artist's work, the authors articulate another benefit: the visual nature of the outline. The outline makes structure visible. Compared to running text, which presents an undifferentiated gray rectangle to the eye, the outline surfaces key topics in an open space, visually demoting subtopics, and showing hierarchical and sequential relationships between the various blocks. Outlining, then, brings some of the resources of the design disciplines to bear on the process of creation. Hacker and Renshaw (1979) emphasize vision: "Your main purpose in writing a sentence outline is to picture the relation between your thesis statement and the major sections of your paper" (p. 107).

For many authors, however, the outline is even more than a two-dimensional layout or sketch. Like clay being molded, it has depth, and the process of creating order out of our notes, impressions, thinking, and reconsiderations can be described as "shaping." Hacker and Renshaw (1979) ring changes on that metaphor: "A paper will probably start to take shape in your head; its shape will become clearer as you scribble on scratch paper and perhaps sketch an outline; then, after you have written the rough draft, you may find yourself reshaping it with numbers and arrows or even with scissors and tape" (p.102). And Johnson (1992) even compares the outline to the first carving of a sculptor: "You can re-search it; that is, review it, and shape it, much as a sculptor creates a form out of marble or wood" (p. 133).

From sculpture, some authors make the leap to planning a building, another form of shaping, but one with more practical appeal. (Perhaps writing outlines seemed too effete, when cloaked in an artist's mantle). Like Bell (1995, p. 80), Brockmann (1986, p. 49), Hacker (1994, p. 30), and Wilcox (1977, p. 65), Wellborn and colleagues (1961) compare the outline with an architectural plan: "An outline is to the writer what a blueprint is to a builder" (p. 54). Thomas (1949) felt uncomfortable with the implications, because builders must follow blueprints exactly, whereas an outline needs to go on changing. "Since the plan for a physical construction shows spatial relations in exact proportion, it necessarily must be precisely followed by the builder. A sentence outline, however, represents logical relations, which are impossible to reduce to an arithmetical scale" (p. 140). Perrin (1955) calls the outline "a working plan, to lay out the material" (p. 13). Hays (1965) expands the metaphor to include specifications and a list of materials: "Writing from an outline is like building from plans, specs, and lists of materials" (p. 100). Similarly, Santmyers (1949) quotes a grateful engineer on the benefits of outlining:"I now see that my trouble with report writing has not been writing, but designing. Frankly, I have not been a good engineer. I have had neither a sketch of the finished product I wanted to build nor a bill of materials with which to work. Of course I fumbled and fussed. But with the limiting sentence to sketch my finished product and the outline as my bill of materials, I can write as an engineer should—with confidence and with measured progress" (p. 46).

Jordan (1965) draws an extended analogy between outlining and designing a building, hesitating to call the outline a blueprint, settling instead for comparing it with an architect's rendering, and emphasizing that even architects change their minds.

> A piece of writing is a **physical structure**, a complex of symbols on paper, designed to evoke in the mind of the reader an intellectual structure....A writer must struggle to embody the mystery of his idea in the substantial form of his essay; and between the germinal thought and the elaborated theme, between the thesis sentence and the finished piece, he needs **architectural assistance**. Such aid is most readily found in a good outline....If you think of an outline as an architect's drawing, you might remember that even architects make mistakes and very few buildings are put up without some changes in plans during construction. (pp.105-106)

So these authors suggest that outlining involves envisioning, seeing in the mind's eye, often in three dimensions (as if all those note cards were trailing off into the background, behind each topic), and then manipulating that structure, most often by moving pieces around, as in modular construction. These authors sometimes seesaw between the fixed nature of a plan and the ongoingness of the structuring activity because they see both aspects of the outline, and fear that students will only see the rigid version as a constraint, and never make enough changes to the outline to get the real benefit—discovering the most effective structure for their purposes.

Looked at another way, these metaphorical descriptions of the process of outlining also suggest that the outline goes through a series of phases, like metal being heated, poured, and hardened. These metaphorical descriptions imply that you are engaged in changing as you sketch, shaping as you go, then hardening the plan into something akin to a blueprint, and finally tinkering with the structure to make it work even better. Although we are talking about outlines—traditionally done early in the composition process, if at all—these descriptions of the way people should revise outlines echo the narratives of professional and literary authors, when describing revisions to their drafts.

In her remarkable survey of the metaphors writers use to describe the way they revise, Tomlinson (1988) sees four stages of revision, based on the changing nature of the document itself. In the first stage, the material is molten enough to reshape; then it hardens, and we can get the parts to work better together; next, the material becomes solid enough that we can cut out unnecessary parts without ruining the whole; and finally, the piece is hard enough to polish, with fine sandpaper and small tools.

Another perspective on the outline is suggested by the authors who compare it to a skeleton. Wicker and Albrecht (1960) say, "An outline is an arrangement in summary or skeleton form of the material the writer proposes to deal with" (p. 51). So at first glance, the writer is assembling the dry bones in an anthropology lab, or analyzing them in the biology lab. Schmidt (1983) justifies the outline as necessary to carry the rest of the material, as the skeleton carries the loose flesh.

> The outline is to the written report as the skeleton is to the human body. Without a skeleton, the body would obviously collapse—and many a piece of writing has sagged or completely caved in because its author did not take the time and trouble to erect a proper scaffolding or skeleton; i.e., a good outline. (pp. 1-11)

So we are at the point at which metaphors of construction (scaffolding) and anatomy (skeleton) coincide. But just how we are to create the skeleton? And how grow flesh around those living bones? Smart and Lang (1943) endeavor to describe the process, continuing with the biological metaphor: "After the outline is completed, the writer is ready for the actual writing of the article. This process consists in filling in the outline by means of details, the different heading serving as nuclei around which the paragraphs in the article are developed" (p. 27).

The body, our familiar model for so much thinking, thus serves to exemplify the relationship between structure and, well, that other stuff—the details, quotes, style, and so on. But a body is also a whole. So this metaphor of an outline as a skeleton, also suggests that an outline lets us create a unity, with nothing sticking out at an odd angle, nothing left out, nothing out of coordination, and components like legs, knees, and toes nicely aligned. Wicker and Albrecht (1960) do not mention the skeleton-with-flesh metaphor, but praise the outline as a way to achieve organic unity.

> Outlines are valuable in two principal ways. First, the outline is synoptic; it permits the writer to view his (sic) material all together, to test it for unity and coherence. Second, it requires the conscientious writer to look at what he is doing and to see his material as an organic pattern. It allows him to discover faulty presentation, wrong proportion or emphasis, gaps or omissions in his thinking, discursiveness (getting off the track or including irrelevant materials), lack of coordination and parallelism between parts, and other defects. (p. 51)

Jordan (1965) quotes Coleridge on "unity in multeity" (p. 115), and in an almost mystical way describes the way a writer moves to incorporate the mystery of his original idea in bodily form—the word made flesh. From that seed, the writer may grow a full and finished form. "A writer must struggle to embody the mystery of his idea in the substantial form of his essay; and between the germinal thought and the elaborated theme, between the thesis sentence and the finished piece, he needs architectural assistance. Such aid is most readily found in a good outline" (p. 105). Jordan stresses the organic nature of the outline, by comparing it with another biological structure, the tree. "Perhaps a good way to overcome the segmental effects of an outline is to think of it not as an artificial and mechanical arrangement of ideas but as a unified organic development. Visualize your outline as a tree rooted in your thesis" (p.116).

With Wicker and Albrecht (1960) and Jordan (1965), then, we have a direct statement of one important entailment of the skeletal metaphor—that to avoid the death of segmentation and mechanical partition, the outline must grow, and through the miracle of spirit in nature, it will grow toward unity, coherence, and parallelism. Once the outline meets those tests, we might say it is mature, and ready to act as the support for the rest of the living material. Not accurate as biology, perhaps, but good enough for a description of the role of an outline, when one thinks of an outline coming before the actual writing. (Of course, in real life and in electronic outlining, the skeleton can form a vital part of the growing body of the draft itself).

Another metaphor, comparing the outline to a map or city plan, brings a different, and later, set of entailments. Now the authors are no longer considering the process of creating the outline; the writer has an outline in hand, and is using it to start writing. The textbooks envision a person sitting down to write a draft, wondering where to start, and how to get through the material, and where to conclude. In this scenario, the outline acts as a map, so the writer does not get detoured, lost, or confused. Schubert (1948) for instance emphasizes the danger that the writer may get lost:

> If you've ever tried to find your way around an unfamiliar city, you know how difficult the job can be. When you stand on the corner of Main and Division Streets, you can be completely lost even though your destination, the corner of High and State Streets, is only a couple of blocks away. If you could magically elevate yourself a few hundred feet so that you could take in the whole area at a glance, you would see the exact relation between Main and Division and High and State. A map of the city would do just as well and would be more practical....If there's a plan and you're familiar with it, you'll have no trouble finding your way around. (p. 135)

So writing, based on an outline, is a matter of moving briskly down the right paths, according to plan. Notice how fixed and firm the outline seems to Santmyers (1949), as if set in print: "Complete Outline. The analysis of your subject is now complete. You know where you are going, what route you are to follow, and the landmarks along the road. You are prepared to set up your orderly scheme in permanent form on a sheet of paper" (p. 35).

Mills and Walter (1962) agree, and emphasize the confusion many young writers feel when they start writing, while dramatizing and justifying the teacher's own bewilderment when reading the students' messy documents.

> Why write an outline? Well, why follow a road map? Probably you have driven a car in a strange city for which you had no map, and after turning around and retracing your route a few times, and after asking pedestrians for information, you have finally pulled up to your destination. Writing is often like that. The writer rushes off first in one direction and then another, while the bewildered reader tries to make sense of his tangled trail. A "road map" would have saved time for both writer and reader. (p. 44)

Other textbook authors (Alred et al., 1992, p. 111; Brusaw et al., 1993, p. 485, Shelton, 1995, p. 39; Weisman, 1962, p. 260) concur with this narrative, imagining the students as writers walking or driving through the points on the outline, blessed with extra speed because it saves them from going off the road. Bell (1995) says "A good working outline can be looked upon as a map of sorts. Using it can remind you where to go next and can ensure that you get from Point A to Point B to Point C as directly as possible" (p. 100).

Schubert (1948) even urges the writer to reveal the plan to the audience, because "it serves as a map to the report" (p. 136). So a reader, too, is conceived of as trying to move through the material, but occasionally getting lost—unless the writer adds the outline to act as a guide. As Weisman (1962) says, the outline "offers the reader guideposts or road signs in the form of heads and subheads" (p. 261).

All these metaphors for the process and purpose of outlining throw some glamour on outlining, borrowed from art, architecture, construction, biology, cartography, geography—in effect, from disciplines that have more interesting reputations than composition or technical writing. However, at a deeper level, these metaphors do articulate important reasons for outlining, entailments that the authors clearly felt happier communicating by implication than by direct statement. To sum up these entailments:

1. Outlining helps the writer visualize structure.
2. As one works on the outline, one starts with very rough (and erasable) sketches, manipulates the basic shape, then modifies the parts, and finally cuts unnecessary elements.

3. The outline is a plan for writing, but the plan can keep on changing.
4. The outline helps the writer unify the material.
5. One grows an outline at the same time as the details of one's thought, and both continue to grow, the outline acting as the structure on which one hangs the rest of the ideas.
6. Once one has an outline in hand, it can keep one from getting lost as one writes.

Such entailments take us way beyond the idea that an outline emerges from the application of "logical" methods, such as dividing, grouping, and sequencing the material. Perhaps the authors chose metaphor as a persuasive strategy that would not conflict with their own earlier reasoning—at least not directly. This way, the authors can call outlining both logical and artistic, verbal and visual, a fixed structure and an evolving meaning—without directly facing the fact that these different representations of outlining cannot be yoked together by logic, although the poetic process accommodates them all.

Metaphors, then, seem to reveal important additional information about outlines—entailing ideas that counter the impressions many students have, such as the idea that outlining is just a horrible torture, that one attempt is enough for an outline, that the outline is just a mess of topics, with no particular relevance to a main point, that an outline should be frozen as soon as it's done, and must then act as a plan the writer can never deviate from, or the instructor will issue a bad grade. In short, by implication, students suffer from a superficial understanding of the process, and these metaphors attempt to show what lies underneath the surface. Oddly, when authors turn to metaphor, they approach deeper, but less easily articulated, truths about the benefits of outlining: its visual nature, its ongoingness, its malleability, its vitality as a structure that grows into a meaningful unity, and its reassuring clarity, as a guide through the confusion of our own thought.

CONCLUSION

Outlining, then, emerges as an activity that engages our reasoning powers, even if it rarely achieves the rigorousness of formal logic. To make a document express one's views on a subject of some complexity one must expect to revise the structure, and outlining appears to be an important way to re-envision that structure, reorganizing the material in a visual hierarchy, because exploring the visual array is more efficient than trying to make the same changes while looking at the undifferentiated flowing text of a draft. Such a process requires taking the outline through many versions. Over time, the structure becomes more internally consistent. The outline, as a document, takes on a lively meaning of its own, so that, as a representative of one's own earlier thoughts, it can lead one through the distracting details of an actual draft. Such, then, is the consensus of the textbook authors, arguing their case for outlining, to the audience of students and other teachers. The persuasive presentation of these ideas suggests the psychological, social, and disciplinary situations the authors imagined themselves in, and the rhetorical strategies they thought would be most effective as they carried out this extended conversation with students through the medium of the book. But these arguments on behalf of outlining also offer common ground between the paper model and the electronic model, if we disregard some of the hyperbole—benefits on which both models can agree.

NOTES

[1] Alvarez, 1980, p. 157; Brusaw et al., 1993, p. 485; Damerst, 1982, p. 59; Dietrich and Brooks, 1958, pp. 109-111; Elsbree & Bracher, 1967, p. 39; Fowler et al., 1992, p. 39; Hacker, 1994, p. 46; Hacker & Renshaw, 1979, p. 107; Harwell, 1960, pp. 122-123; Hays, 1965, p. 104; Johnson, 1992, p. 141; Jordan, 1965, pp. 108-111; Leggett et al., 1960, pp. 196-197; Lester, 1990, p. 114; Marckwardt & Cassidy, 1960, p. 408; Markel, 1984, p. 70; Mills & Walter, 1962, p. 45; Rubens, 1992, p. 15; Shelton, 1995, p. 42; Sherman, 1955, p. 12 and 1966, p. 34; Smart & Lang, 1943, pp. 19-26; Thomas, 1949, pp. 130-142; Weiss, 1982, p. 52; Wellborn et al., 1961, p. 55; Wicker & Albrecht, 1960, p. 54; Wilcox, 1977, pp. 83-86.

[2] Crews, 1980, p. 74; Elsbree & Bracher, 1967, pp. 30, 42-43; Fowler et al., 1992, pp. 39-40; Johnson, 1992, pp. 141-143; Jordan, 1965. p. 110; Leggett et al., 1960, p. 201; Mansfield & Bahniuk, 1981, p. 268; Marckwardt & Cassidy, 1960, pp. 410-411; Mills & Walter, 1962, p. 45, and1978, pp. 55-60; Naylor, 1942, pp. 48-49; Pearsall & Cunningham, 1978, p. 272; Perrin, 1955, p. 674; Santmyers, 1949, p. 31; Sherman, 1955, pp. 12-13; Smart & Lang, 1943, p. 26; Thomas, 1949, pp. 132-135; Trzyna & Batschelet, 1987, pp. 98, 103; Weiss, 1982, p. 51; Wellborn & Nall, 1961, p. 56; Wicker & Albrecht, 1960, pp. 54-58; Wilcox, 1977, p. 87.

III

Summing Up

6
Toward a New Model of Outlining

E veryone agrees that structure is important, though few care to define it very precisely. Somehow, the structure of a document indicates what the author imagines the audience may want to know first, second, and third, what may be most important to them, or less so, and what sequence of topics may be most meaningful to them. Structure allows fast access, or forestalls it; encourages people to move through the document with confidence, or discourages them from reading more. Overall, the structure makes the material meaningful, memorable, and usable.

So rhetoricians, composition teachers, and instructors of technical communication have all insisted that their students consider a series of different structures as they develop their material, switching topics around, deleting some, adding others, in order to settle on the most effective structure for a particular document, in a particular situation. The mechanism most commonly recommended for this important work is the outline.

However, although these teachers and textbook authors rarely want to admit it, the medium of paper has made outlining difficult, tedious, and mechanical. And, without most people recognizing it, that medium has also shaped their conception of the times when one ought to outline, the product of that work, and the relationship between the outline and other documents, such as notes, drafts, and revisions. This nexus of ideas, I believe, limited the benefits writers got out of outlining. Hence, student and adult writers developed resentments, leading to resistance or downright refusal to do anything but the most trivial outlines. In response, the textbook authors have come up with a series of arguments in favor of creating a paper outline, based on its supposed logic, practicality, and malleability, as a writer moves toward a fuller vision of the material.

But electronic outlining—creating an outline on the computer and working with it onscreen—has now been widely available in America for more than a dozen years. Noticed and used more by professional writers than by teachers or students, this tool allows us a new understanding of outlining, and, ultimately, of structure. In business and government, technical writing teams, overwhelmed by the volume of work to be done, have turned to many forms of electronic document creation and management, including the electronic outliner. Perhaps such software appeals more to this group because they generally have to write several full-length books at once, under extremely tight deadlines, with changing information, and many partners at their side.

Whenever a group encounters difficulty achieving its aims with one set of tools and media, it seems, some members may cast about for new tools, new media. But changes in tools and media often enable—or force—this group of pioneers to change the way they interact when they work together to create a document that reflects some mutual understanding. When any technology—whether note cards, theme paper, or electronic outlining software—becomes widely available, it also becomes a visible symbol, or working metaphor, that all members of the community can use to extend their thinking about the way they build meaning together. For instance, Derrida (1973, 1981, 1986) and Barthes (1974, 1982, 1984) recognized intertextuality, but hypertext displays it. Social constructionists saw how a discipline develops as intertext, and how even one person's work is, as Bakhtin (1981, 1989) noted, a social process. But new tools such as email, web sites, document management software, hypertext editors, word processing, and electronic outlining allow more people to work together more visibly, and because of that very visibility, these new tools can, with a little help, accelerate people's thinking about the social nature of the way we create meaning together. New tools often allow us to rethink familiar activities, because we can do some aspects of the activities somewhat more effectively, though differently. The change in perspective may also help us see more clearly the original purposes, and, with a little luck, discover new work we can accomplish, tasks we may never have imagined before.

But at the same time that new tools and media are adopted by one part of the discourse community as described by Bizzell (1982), Faigley (1985), and Porter, (1986), another group usually remains unconvinced, devoted to earlier media, and, even if they must use some of the new technology, they continue to use concepts developed from the activities and artifacts of the earlier medium. With some of these textbooks, I believe, we see the authors in that odd situation, using word processing to produce the books, but still thinking with concepts that reflect paper, as a medium. For instance, many of the authors think in terms of a series of stages, and discrete documents, such as notes, outline, first draft, final draft, whereas electronically, a single file may contain an outline view, notes that are hidden or revealed, as necessary, and a word processing view of the full text. The school model of outlining represents a kind of cultural lock-in (Arthur, 1990, 1996), leading even open-minded experimenters with hypertext or the World Wide Web to hesitate before returning to that scene of teenage resentments, the outline.

Outlining has been generally ignored in critical discussions carried on in the fields of technical communication, composition, and rhetoric. Textbooks, though, present outlining as a practical tool, and many instructors teach the practice, with varying degrees of enthusiasm. Perhaps future textbook authors will take a more balanced approach, considering the electronic model as an alternative to the school, or paper, model.

In this book, we have looked at outlining critically, and gradually discerned two models of outlining, based on the medium in which one works. Let me summarize the differences in tabular form, then draw out the implications, as I see them. In Table 1, I contrast the way the two models conceptualize attributes of the outline itself, and the process of outlining.

TABLE 1. Two Models of Outlining

Paper Model	Electronic Model
The Outline Itself	
The outline is a paper document.	The outline is an electronic file, capable of being stored for reuse, printed on paper, or reworked on the fly (in the computer's memory).
The outline is the result of research and thought.	The outline is a snapshot of an ongoing process, preserving and encouraging further thinking about the research.
The outline is a document that is distinct from notes and drafts.	The outline offers one view into the file, which is a single locus for note-taking, planning, and drafting (an alternate to the layout, text, and hypertext views).

(continued)

TABLE 1.   Continued

Paper Model	Electronic Model
The Outline Itself (continued)	
The outline is a fixed blueprint or map for a future draft.	The outline is an evolving structure within which the draft is already growing, in bits and pieces; not closed, final, or finished, just abandoned at some point.
The outline presents fixed hierarchy and sequence of topics.	The outline shows the current status of an evolving hierarchy and sequence of topics.
The outline depends on a limited number of formats to distinguish levels (labels, indentation, occasionally capitalization and size); formatting allows structure to be deduced, if done carefully enough by the writer.	The outlining software uses whole range of word-processing formats to give each level a distinct look; automatically dramatizes the structure, visually.
Labeling generally indicates that the topics must appear in a sequence (1, 2, 3; a, b, c).	Bullets and non-sequential labeling are possible for topics that are simply options, or alternatives, and do not have to appear in a particular order.
The outline is intended for the use of the writer (and perhaps a teacher, monitoring progress). No one else will see it.	The outline is intended for the use of the writer (or writing team) and, as a menu system or electronic table of contents, for end users.
The outline is a personal tool, allowing for limited consideration of alternate structures, then frozen, as a blueprint for the draft.	The outline is a focal point for extended internal considering and collaborative conversation with other people.
Making an outline saves time and money, because it keeps the writer on track when drafting the actual document.	Making an outline is a continuous process that improves the quality of the document for the end user, and, incidentally, saves the writer time, particularly toward the end of a hectic project, when the extensive reviews pay off in fewer requests for structural change.
The outline document may take one of various forms, or a sequence of them (scratch notes, nonlinear diagrams, lists, numbered lists, preliminary outline, working outline, sentence outline, paragraph outline)	The outline tends to evolve from a list to a hierarchy with many levels, each with its own sequencing; the topics become headings, and the lower levels become sentences, then paragraphs, within the same file. The outline is always a working document.
The first outline, seen artistically, is a rough sketch, a tentative plan that helps us distinguish structure because it stands out visually, compared to running text.	The outline is always a work in progress, and like an artist's sketch, exposes key aspects of the composition through color, position, and format.

(continued)

TABLE 1.   Continued

Paper Model	Electronic Model

The Outline Itself (continued)

The outline acquires the appearance of depth, becoming a three-dimensional model we can shape and then use when we write the draft.	The outlining tool lets you move up and down, and, through showing what was hidden, in. These three dimensions give the electronic outline a feeling of depth like that of a hypertext Help system or CD-ROM, in which we move through the environment.
The outline is a scaffolding for the building to come (the draft), or bones for a body to emerge around them.	The outline may act as a menu system by which users navigate through the material; in that sense, some users imagine the menu system as a kind of three-dimensional array through which they are moving. For the writer, the growing outline does sometime seem like a skeleton on which the organs hang, and around which the flesh of text grows.
The outline is a map, guiding the writer of the draft.	The outline acts as a series of maps of the material, allowing the writer to zoom in from a high-level view to a medium-level view to a closeup. At any level, the emerging outline helps the writer stay oriented.

The Activities of Outlining

Consolidating what has been learned, during research.	Discovering meaning in what has been found so far, noticing gaps in our knowledge, using the structuring process as a way to learn.
Comparing the outline with the notes, to verify accuracy and completeness.	Opening and closing, showing and revealing notes to verify accuracy and completeness; also showing and hiding lower levels of headings, and partial drafts, for the same purposes.
Creating one final structure (a hierarchy and sequence of topics).	Continuously improving a structure (a hierarchy and sequence of topics).
Requiring no real writing, except to enforce parallelism, because the outline is considered "just a plan," and not part of the final document.	Allowing, even requiring that the writer do real writing from the beginning, so that the headings make sense as a menu, and as a summary.
Revising by crossing out, inserting, drawing arrows, then recopying the entire outline to get a clean copy.	Revising without any recopying of the materials that have not been changed, because reformatting is automatic, and you always see a clean copy.

(continued)

TABLE 1.   Continued

Paper Model	Electronic Model
The Activities of Outlining (continued)	
Applying logic, particularly the activities of division, grouping, and sequencing	Using the outline as a tool to represent our current understanding, allowing us to view that critically, and rethink it, or research the gaps in our knowledge.
Transforming a sketch, manipulating a basic shape, modifying parts, cutting away the unnecessary.	Directly manipulating the first list as it becomes a hierarchical shape, constantly modifying the parts and cutting away the unnecessary.
Growing together organically, to form a unified, living whole.	Constantly moving toward greater unity by eliminating discordant elements, conflicts, duplication, ambiguity; when placed in an electronic environment, the outline becomes hot, that is, interactive, because clicking a topic takes the user to a submenu or page of information.
Applying a limited set of activities (three or four, according to most authors), out of the many recognized as possible: identifying and making a list of topics, adding or deleting topics, moving topics, eliminating duplicate topics, classifying or grouping, dividing one topic into subtopics, subordinating some topics to others, sequencing, confirming completeness, rewriting to emphasize similarity, working on one layer at a time	Involves many overlapping and interacting activities, in many cycles: identifying and making a list of topics, adding or deleting topics, moving topics, annotating topics, deleting duplicate topics, dividing one topic into its components, creating a new topic out of the details, disassembling a set of subtopics, promoting a subtopic or demoting a topic, grouping, sequencing, rewriting to emphasize similarity and difference, rewriting to reveal structure, writing test passages, and drafts, verifying that similar topics have similar subtopics, confirming completeness.
Giving particular attention to activities that lead to an essay: including an introduction, starting with a thesis statement, ensuring that headings support the thesis, and including a conclusion.	Allowing any structure, including that of the formal essay, but not insisting on inserting an introduction, thesis, or conclusion into every document.
Tending to fix on a particular structure, and refine that, without extensive consideration of alternatives.	Involving constant comparison of various structures
Making a limited number of passes, due to the tedium of recopying.	Making countless versions; revising continuously, from the first note through the final draft.

(continued)

TABLE 1.   Continued

Paper Model	Electronic Model
The Activities of Outlining (continued)	
Fixing the structure, so it is all open and revealed at once, making some comparisons difficult.	Through hiding and showing, allowing movement through the structure at different levels, under different topics, and in different sequences, for multiple comparisons.
Making a new outline as a diagnostic tool to analyze the structure of a draft.	Always offering an outline view, even during the final draft, because the outline is just another view of the same file as the draft, allowing constant comparison between structure and text
During the writing of the draft, if new ideas occur, incorporating them into the draft only, or forcing a new revision of the outline.	Slipping new ideas into the evolving outline whenever they occur, even during drafting or revising the draft.
To analyze the structure of a draft, making another outline.	To analyze the structure of a draft, the writer simply shifting to outline view.
Learning takes place before outlining; the outline serves to summarize that, or incorporate future thoughts.	Working on the outline is a way of learning the material, and interrogating one's own earlier view of the structure, and therefore, the meaning.
The outline acts as a substitute for short-term memory, preserving the structure for analysis, reconsideration, and possibly another version of the outline, or, at any rate, for the next document (the draft).	The outline is a tool for talking to oneself and others about the material; a temporary artifact holding the individual's last thought, or the group's last consensus, for analysis and improvement.
The outline reflects the writer's thoughts, belongs to the writer, retains the writer's individual signature.	When a group is outlining, the ideas become the property of the group, and individual contributions tend to lose their signatures.
When considered as an individual activity, the outlining process looks like problem-solving, or some other form of individual thinking, distanced from the influence of others (their thoughts, in summary, survive only in the note cards).	When considered as a group activity, the outlining process reflects the social construction of meaning.

What a difference the medium makes! The school model is heavily, if unconsciously, influenced by the tradition of paper: index cards, typed sheets, stacks of notes. The assumption that one must use paper to outline encouraged authors to think of making an outline as a difficult but limited stage a writer had to go through, yielding a single discrete document that could act as a map to the essay as it was written.

With the arrival of word processing and electronic software we can begin to look at outlining as an ongoing process involving a whole set of iterative, nonsequential, but overlapping activities, some of which have traditionally been done to prepare an outline, such as promoting or demoting topics, while others used to be considered distinctly different stages (researching, writing, revising), and still others were not even considered relevant to outlining (collaborative construction of meaning). By contrast to the classic paper outline, the electronic outline then, is always open, ready for further change, unfinished and full of potential. At the beginning of the outlining process, we may do more reading, and at the end, more tinkering with words, but we never stop either activity completely, at least not on a major project. We proceed by bits and pieces. We do a little research, we synthesize that, we write a little about it, we realize we need to do more reading, we edit the paragraph we wrote, we think…and so it goes. How illogical we are—and how holistic! We do not take the straight road to the final document, we meander. We do not go by stages, we cycle through different activities, day after day, gradually changing our emphasis as our ideas get clear, and we discover what we are doing.

The complex and iterative nature of the process suggests that when outlining works, it is not an isolated act, with a discrete product, but is an important part of an ongoing writing process, linked to all other aspects of that process. And with electronic outlining, all these activities can operate in the same file, allowing us to shift in an instant from an activity focused on notes to an activity at the highest level, considering structure in the outline. In order to move the material from a simple list to a complete document, we constantly cycle through different views of the evolving file: the outline view, the text view, the page layout view, and the hypertext, Web, or linked view. Because our electronic tools allow such quick switching from one view to another, they also help us see the extent to which writing is a complex process, made up of so many sub-processes that interact so unpredictably with each other that we can never hope to describe all the activities that go into a single book, much less prescribe a particular sequence of activities for a writer to follow when creating an outline. At best we can regard outlining as part of an extended set of conversations.

Several conversations drive the onrushing flow of these activities. The first conversation is between the writer and his or her own artifact, the outline as it now stands, needing to be shaped by further thought; in this sense, the outline externalizes interior dialog. The second conversation draws in the documents the writer has consulted, debated, argued with, and borrowed from. The third conversation is between the author, the emerging document, and its intended audiences, who, though absent, keep speaking up, raising questions, wondering, doubting, and generally provoking the writer to further effort. When the outline appears in electronic form, it is just one view of a document that can also be looked at in unending scroll, as a word processing document, or in distinct pages, as a desktop publishing document, or again in a hierarchical outline, so we no longer seem to be looking at a single completed document, but rather a moment's snapshot, a brief recording or digest of all the ongoing conversations.

In the workplace and the classroom, the electronic outline also dramatizes the social construction of knowledge, encouraging collaborative work among a team or class, foregrounding the processes of negotiation, problem-solving, reorganizing, and eventual agreement. As an artifact of these multiple ongoing conversations, then, the outline also acts as an object of contemplation, a temporary but material representation of the talk, allowing participants to step back for a moment, and reflect on the way in which they are all, jointly, participating in the creation of this shared document.

When we regard the outline in this way, we begin to see that each element in it—each heading, each section—functions as the collective writers' best attempt to answer a particular question, or set of questions from the various audiences. In addition, each element may send a message, as it were, to another part of the outline; the introduction to a chapter, for instance, presages the body, and the summary looks back to both. The document can be viewed as a hierarchy built out of these elements, and, similarly, any top-level element can be seen as containing other elements, as its components. All headings at one level belong to that class of headings, and, in a formally designed document, each gets the same format as its peers, but each is also a distinct instance of the class, having its own data, or content. In all these ways, an electronic outline, particularly one with hypertext links within and without, is an object-oriented document, as a software engineer might describe it (Mazumdar et al., 1998; Price 1997a, 1997b, 1998). And when the document is presented electronically, the outline itself becomes a multi-level menu system, allowing users to traverse the material by various paths, interrogating the topic hierarchies and sequences, directing the conversation toward their own ends, creating their own meanings.

In large organizations we already see document creation and management moving in this direction, as software vendors perfect tools for flowcharting, color-coding and formatting the levels in a programmer's code so it looks like an outline, schematic diagramming, and visualization, as well as document-building tools based on the Standard General Markup Language, or SGML, and its subset XML, which allow each team to create its own standard outline for a set of documents, displaying that template next to the document, in effect nudging the individual writers to observe the structural necessities imposed by the team's description of the ideal document of this type (in the document-type description, or DTD). By separating format from structure, these new electronic tools take outlining even farther from the "paper plan," and foreground the collaborative nature of the creation.

This sophisticated version of electronic outlining helps us understand structure in a new way—as an assemblage of message-sending objects in an evolving hierarchy, with each object having its own function in the virtual conversation for which the document acts as a continuous mediator. The structure of a document, then, can no longer be considered a stable scaffolding. Viewed electronically, the emerging structure acts as a communicating system linking several societies, facilitating the complex social process of conversation (Price, 1997a, 1997b, 1998).

Having looked at the paper model and the electronic model, we are inclined to ask: So what does this analysis tell us of outlining in general? The answer is that there is no such beast.

Each medium enables and encourages some activities, discourages others, and makes some almost impossible. As we work in the medium regularly, our common activities shape the types of documents that normally emerge, the ideas that we have about these documents, and the way we conceive of the rhetorical exchange and the process we have gone through. The electronic medium inherited a range of possible structuring activities but shifted the priorities, multiplied the number of passes, increased the interactions between activities exponentially. Similarly, certain design motifs continue, such as indentations and labels, but the rest of the formatting becomes visually more sophisticated, clarifying many aspects of structure that were not easy to spot before, and offering dramatic changes in what we see from moment to moment. We recognize traces of the idea of a document, but now it is more file than paper, so different attributes rise to the surface. The internal dialog becomes externalized in a new way, and other people join in. There is, then, no generic outlining, because medium is determinative in the definition.

We may pursue an idea through many media, but each process and each document emerges deeply stained by its own medium—and we humans seem to like it that way. Viewed in this light, the shift to a new medium and new tools—a new communication technology—is driven by a wide range of social, economic, and intellectual choices, but beneath all those decisions, I see a very human yearning for greater shared understanding.

CONCLUSION

In the process of outlining, then, we use an external medium to hammer out the structure of complex thought in verbal and visual form. The outline itself is a momentary snapshot, recording a structural perspective on our writing up to that point, often incorporating what we have learned from research and what we have drafted so far, but presenting the topics in a visual hierarchy and sequence dramatized by design elements such as spatial layout in lines, paragraphs, laid out vertically and horizontally, and reenforced by variations in labels, font, color, and size. Compared to notes, running text, formatted text, and hypertext versions of the document, the outline, then, is simply one view among many of the evolving information. It may be consulted whenever we sense an internal inconsistency in our thought, add an idea that we had not anticipated, feel the need for clearer orientation in our research or drafting, or realize we must polish our thinking in particular locations, or throughout the document.

Because the outline fixes our ideas temporarily, we can interrogate and revise the organization at many scales, from focussing on a single point to canvassing the top-level ideas. Such objectification of our thought allows interior conversation with our most recent concepts, unburdened by any need to remember everything in our heads. Bringing common mental strategies to bear on the evolving artifact, cyclically, in many overlapping and interacting passes, we gradually unify and articulate our conception of the subject—learning as we go. Adding the voices of people whose work we take notes on, we extend the conversation, using the outline to place their thoughts within our own evolving vision. And practicing outlining with other people, we engage in collaborative brainstorming, analysis, and creation—if the medium can keep up with the flow. Outlining together allows each person full participation, but gradually erases claims to ownership, so that the process begins to seem simply an extensive, ongoing conversation, with shared results.

The media chosen—and to a lesser extent, the tools used to manipulate that medium—affect outlining by encouraging or discouraging, enabling or making difficult, the externalization of our evolving thought as we come to understanding a subject structurally. The media and tools available—the communication technologies—exist along a range from slowest to fastest, from most recalcitrant to most flexible, from least legible to most visible, from difficult to modify to easy, even fluid. In our own era, we have seen outlining on a blackboard, on paper, and on the computer, but because outlining cannot exist without a medium, its nature changes as it moves from one medium to another, expanding and deepening all our conversations.

References

Adelson, N., & Jordan, T. (1992). The need for negotiation in cooperative work. In E. Barrett (Ed.), *Sociomedia: Multimedia, hypermedia, and the social construction of knowledge* (pp. 469-492). Cambridge, MA: MIT.

Agger, B. (1992). *Cultural studies as critical theory*. London: Oxford University Press.

Allen, N., Atkinson, D., Morgan, M., Moore, T., & Snow, C. (1987). What experienced collaborators say about collaborative writing. *Journal of Business and Technical Communication, 1*, 70-90.

Alred, G., Oliu, W., & Brusaw, C. (1992). *The professional writer: A guide for advanced technical writing*. New York: St. Martin's Press.

Alvarez, J. (1980). *Elements of technical writing*. New York: Harcourt Brace Jovanovich.

Anderson, S. L., Campbell, C., Hindle, N., Price, J., & Scasny, R. (1998). Editing a website: Extending the levels of edit. *IEEE Transactions in Professional Communication, 41*, 47-57.

Andrews, C. (1975). *Technical and business writing*. Boston: Houghton Mifflin.

Andrews, D., & Blickle, M. (1982). *Technical writing: Principles and forms*. New York: Macmillan.

Apple Computer (1987). *Apple human interface guidelines: The Apple desktop interface*. Reading, MA: Addison Wesley.

Apple, M. W. (1986). *Teachers and texts: A political economy of class and gender relations in education*. New York, Routledge & Kegan Paul.

Arthur, W. B. (1990). Positive feedbacks in the economy. *Scientific American*, February. 92-99.

Arthur, W. B. (1996) Increasing returns and the two worlds of business. (Working Paper for Santa Fe Institute Research Program 96-05-028). Santa Fe, NM: Santa Fe Institute.

Baker, W. H. (1994). How to produce and communicate structured text. *Technical Communication, 41*, 456-466.

Bakhtin, M. M. (1981).*The dialogic imagination: Four essays by M. M. Bakhtin*. (M. Holquist, Ed., C. Emerson & M. Holquist, Trans.). Austin, TX: University of Texas Press.

Bakhtin, M. M. (1986). *Speech genres and other late essays*. (C. Emerson & M. Holquist, Eds., V. W. McGee, Trans.). Austin, TX: University of Texas Press.

Bakhtin, M., & Volosinov, V. N. (1986/1929). *Marxism and the philosophy of language*. (L. Matejka & I. Titunik, Trans.). Cambridge, MA: Harvard.

Balestri, D. P. (1988). Softcopy and hard: Word processing and writing process. *Academic Computing*, 14-17, 41-45.

Barrett, E. (1988). Introduction: A new paradigm for writing with and for the computer. In E. Barrett (Ed.), *Text, conText, and hyperText: Writing with and for the computer*, pp. xiii-xxv.. Cambridge, MA: MIT.

Barrett, E. (1989). Textual intervention, collaboration, and the online environment. In E. Barrett (Ed.), *The society of text: Hypertext, hypermedia, and the social construction of information*, pp. 227-249. Cambridge, MA: MIT.

Barrett, E., & Paradis, J. (1988). Teaching writing in an on-line classroom. *Harvard Education Review*, *58*, 154-71.

Barthes, R. (1974/1970). *S/Z: An essay*. (R. Miller, Trans.). New York: Hill & Wang.

Barthes, R. (1982/1970). *Empire of signs*. (R. Howard, Trans.). New York: Farrar, Straus, & Giroux.

Barthes, R. (1986/1971). From work to text. In R. Howard (Trans.), *The Rustle of Language*. New York: Hill & Wang.

Barton, E. L. (1994). Interpreting the discourses of technology. In C. L. Selfe & S. Hilligoss (Eds.), *Literacy and computers: The complications of teaching and learning with technology* (pp. 56-75). New York: Modern Language Association.

Batschelet, M. W. (1988). Plain style and scientific style: The influence of the Puritan plain style sermon on early American science writers. *Journal of Technical Writing and Communication*, *18*, 287-295.

Baudrillard, J. (1983). *Simulations*. (Trans. P. Foss, P. Patton, & P. Beitchman). New York: Semiotext(e).

Baugh, L. S. (1993). *How to write term papers and reports*. Lincolnwood, IL: VGM Career Horizons.

Bazerman, C. (1994). *Constructing experience*. Carbondale, IL: Southern Illinois University Press.

Beach, R. (1976). Self-evaluation strategies of extensive reviewers and non-revisers. *College Composition and Communication*, *34*, 297-312.

Beaugrande, R. de. (1984). *Text production*. Norwood, NJ: Ablex.

Beaugrande, R. de, & Dressler, W. (1981). *Introduction to text linguistics*. New York: Longman.

Bell, A. H. (1995). *Tools for technical and professional communication*. Lincolnwood, IL: NTC Publishing.

Bell, D. (1975). The social framework of the information society. In M. Dertouzos & J. Moses (Eds). *The computer age: A twenty-year view* (pp. 163-211). Cambridge, MA: MIT.

Bereiter, C., & Scardamalia, M. (1987). *The psychology of written composition*. Hillsdale, NJ: Erlbaum.

Bernhardt, S. A. (1986). Seeing the text. *College Composition and Communication, 37,* 66-78.

Bernhardt, S. A., Edwards, P., & Wojahn, P. (1989). Teaching college composition with computers: A program evaluation. *Written Communication, 6,* 108-133.

Bilsky, M., McCrea, H., Streeter, R., & Weaver, R. (1953). Looking for an argument. *College English, 14,* 210-216.

Bizzell, P. (1982). College composition: Initiation into the academic discourse community. *Curriculum Inquiry, 12,* 191-207

Bleich, D. (1995). Collaboration and the pedagogy of disclosure. *College English, 57,* 43-61.

Bliven, B. (1954). *The wonderful writing machine.* New York: Random House.

Bolter, J. D. (1991). *Writing space: The computer, hypertext, and the history of writing.* Hillsdale, NJ: Erlbaum.

Borowick, J. (1996). *Technical communication and its applications.* Englewood Cliffs, NJ: Prentice Hall.

Bradford, A. N. (1983). Cognitive immaturity and remedial college writers. In J. N. Hays, P. A. Roth, J. R. Ramsey, and R. D. Foulke (Eds.), *The writer's mind: Writing as a mode of thinking,* pp. 15-24. Urbana, IL: NCTE.

Brantlinger, P. (1990). *Crusoe's footprints: Cultural studies in Britain and America.* New York: Routledge.

Bridwell, L. S. (1980). Revising strategies in twelfth grade students' transactional writing. *Research in the Teaching of English, 14,* 197-222.

Britton, J., Burgess, T., Martin, N., McLeod, A., & Rosen, H. (1975). *The development of writing abilities.* London: Macmillan.

Brockmann, R. J. (1990). *Writing better computer user documentation: From paper to online, Version 2.0.* New York: Wiley.

Bruffee, K. A. (1983). Writing and reading as collaborative or social acts. In J. N. Hays, P. A. Roth, J. R. Ramsey, & R. D. Foulke (Eds.), *The writer's mind: Writing as a mode of thinking,* pp. 159-169. Urbana, IL: NCTE..

Bruffee, K. A. (1984). Collaborative learning and 'the conversation of mankind.' *College English, 46,* 635-652.

Bruffee, K. A. (1986). Social construction, language, and the authority of knowledge. *College English, 48,* 773-790.

Brusaw, C., Alred, G., & Oliu, W. (1993). *Handbook of technical writing* (Fourth Edition). New York: St Martin's Press.

Burnett, R. E. (1993). Conflict in collaborative decision-making. In N. R. Blyler & C. Thralls (Eds.), *Professional communication: The social perspective* (pp. 144-162). Newbury Park, CA: Sage.

Burnor, R. N. (1995). Outlines for success: Computer outlining and teaching philosphy. *Teaching Philosophy, 18* (1). <http:maxthink.com/max.html> (1998, August 26).

Burtis, P. J., Bereiter, C., Scardamalia, M., & Tetroe, J. (1983). The development of planning in writing. In G. Wells & B. M. Kroll (Eds.), *Explorations in the development of writing* (pp. 153-174). Chichester, UK: John Wiley.

Card, S., Moran, T. P., & Newell, A. (1983). *The psychology of human-computer interaction.* Hillsdale, NJ: Erlbaum.

Carmody, S., Gross, W., Nelson, T. H., Rice, D., & van Dam, A. (1969). A hypertext editing system for the /360." In M. Faiman & J. Nievergetl (Eds.), *Pertinent concepts in computer graphics* (pp. 291-330). Urbana, IL: U of Illinois Press.

Charney, D. (1994). The effect of hypertext on processes of reading and writing. In C. L. Selfe & S. Hilligoss, (Eds.), *Literacy and computers: The complications of teaching and learning with technology* (pp. 238-263). (Research and Scholarship in Composition Series). New York: Modern Language Association.

Chartier, R. (1994/1992). *The order of books: Readers, authors, and libraries in Europe between the fourteenth and eighteenth centuries* (L. G. Cochrane, Trans.). Stanford, CA: Stanford University Press.

Cicero, M. T. (1949/46 B.C.). *De inventione, De optimo genere oratorum, & Topica.* (H. M. Hubbell, Trans.). (Loeb Classical Library #386). Cambridge, MA: Harvard.

Clear, J. H. (1993) The British National Corpus. In G. P. Landow & P. Delany (Eds.), *The digital word: Text-based computing in the humanities* (pp. 163-187). Cambridge, MA: MIT Press.

Coe, R. M. (1981). *Form and substance: An advanced rhetoric.* Glenview, IL: Scott, Foresman.

Coe, R. M. (1987). An apology for form: Or, who took form out of the process? *College English, 49,* 13-28.

Coles, W. E, Jr. (1991). The dialogues of teaching: Learning to listen. *Composition Studies, 12,* 34-46.

Cook, M. A. (1996). *Building enterprise information architectures: Reenginering information systems.* Upper Saddle River, NJ: Prentice Hall.

Coombs, J. H., Renear, A.H., & DeRose, S.J. (1987). Markup systems and the future of scholarly text processing. *Communications of the ACM, 30,* 933-47. Reprinted in G. P. Landow & P. Delany (Eds.) (1993) *The digital word: Text-based computing in the humanities* (pp. 85-118). Cambridge, MA: MIT.

Cooper, M. M., & Selfe, C. L. (1990). Computer conferences and learning: Authority, resistance, and internally persuasive discourse. *College English, 52,* 847-869.

Costanzo, W. (1994). Reading, writing, and thinking in an age of electronic literacy. In C. L. Selfe & S. Hilligoss (Eds.), *Literacy and computers: The complications of teaching and learning with technology* (pp. 11-21) New York: Modern Language Association.

Couture, B., & Rymer, J. (1989). Interactive writing on the job: Definitions and implications of collaboration. In M. Kogen (Ed.), *Writing in the business professions* (pp. 73-93). Urbana, IL: NCTE.

Crawford, W. (1989). Common-sense outline processing. *Library Hi-Tech, 16,* 63-77.

Crews, F. (1980). *The Random House handbook.* New York: Random House.

Daiute, C. (1985). *Writing and computers.* Reading, MA: Addison-Wesley.

Daiute, C. (1986). Do 1 and 1 make 2?: Patterns of influence by collaborative authors. *Written Communication, 3,* 382-408.

Damerst, W. (1982).*Clear technical reports.* New York: HBJ Media Systems.

Danforth, S. (1665). *An astronomical description of the late comet or blazing star as it appeared in New-England in the 9th, 10th, 11th, and in the beginning of the 12th moneth (sic), 1664. Together with a brief theological application thereofe.* Cambridge, MA: Samuel Green.

Darnton, J. (1966, June 15). House is given its due: Darwin cogitated here, with photographs by J. Player. *The New York Times*, International Section, p. 4.

Darwin, C. (1889). Letter. In F. Darwin (Ed.), *The life and letters of Charles Darwin.* New York: Appleton.

Davis, R. M. (1977). How important is technical writing? A survey of the opinions of successful engineers. *Technical Writing Teacher, 4,* 83-88.

DeKoven, B. (1995). The fun factor in groupware design and implementation. <http:\\www.california.com\fun\funfactr.htm> (1998, August 3).

DeKoven, B. (1998a). Secrets of technography. <http:\\www.california.com\fun\secrets.htm> (1998, August 3).

DeKoven, B. (1998b). Welcome to the In Formation age. <http:\\www.california.com\fun\in_form.htm> (1998, August 3).

Derrida, J. (1973). *Speech and phenomena* (D.B. Allison, Trans.). Evanston, IL: Northwestern University Press.

Derrida, J. (1981/1972). *Dissemination* (B. Johnson, Trans.). Chicago, IL: University of Chicago Press.

Derrida, J. (1986/1974). *Glas* (J.P. Leavey, Jr. & R. Rand, Trans.). Lincoln, NB: University of Nebraska Press.

Dietrich, J., & Brooks, K. (1958). *Practical speaking for the technical man.* Englewood Cliffs, NJ: Prentice-Hall.

Dobrin, D. N. (1987). Some ideas about idea processors. In L. Gerrard (Ed.), *Writing at century's end: Essays on computer-assisted composition* (pp. 95-107). New York: Random House.

Duin, A.H. (1991). Computer-supported collaborative writing: The workplace and the writing classroom. *Journal of Business and Technical Communication, 5,* 123-150.

Duin, A. H., & Burnett, R. (1993). Collaboration in technical communication: A research continuum. *Technical Communication Quarterly, 2,* 5-21.

Duin, A. H. & Hansen, C. (1994). Reading and writing on computer networks as social construction and social interaction. In C. L. Selfe, & S. Hilligoss (Eds.), *Literacy and computers: The complications of teaching and learning with technology* (pp. 89-112). New York: Modern Language Association.

Ede, L., & Lunsford, A. (1986). Why write...together: A research update. *Rhetoric Review, 5,* 71-81.

Ede, L., & Lunsford, A. (1990). *Singular texts/Plural authors: Perspectives on collaborative writing.* Carbondale, IL: Southern Illinois University Press.

Ehrlich, E., & Murphy, D. (1964).*Writing and researching term papers and reports: A new guide for students.* New York: Bantam.

Elbow, P. (1981). *Writing with power.* New York: Oxford.

Eldred, J. M. (1989). Computers, composition pedagogy, and the social view. In G. E. Hawisher & C. L. Selfe (Eds.) *Critical perspectives on computers and composition instruction* (pp. 201-218). New York: Teachers' College Press.

Elsbree, L., & Bracher, F. (1967). *Heath's college handbook of composition*. Boston: D.C. Heath.

Emig, J. (1971). *The composing processes of twelfth graders*. (Research Report No. 13). Urbana, IL: National Council of Teachers of English.

Engelbart, D. C., & English, W. K. (1968). A research center for augmenting human intellect. In I. Greif (Ed.), *Computer-supported cooperative work: A book of readings* (pp. 81-105). San Mateo, CA: Morgan Kaufmann.

Enos, R. L. (1985). Ciceronian *dispositio* as an architecture for creativity in composition: A note for the affirmative. *Rhetoric Review, 4*, 108-110.

Erasmus, D. (1990/1512). De copia. In C. R. Thompson (Ed.), *Collected works of Eramus: Literary and educational writings 2: De copia. De ratione studii*, 1978 (B. I. Knott, Trans.) Excerpted in P. Bizzell & B. Herzberg (Eds.), *The Rhetorical Tradition* (pp. 502-556). Boston: Bedford.

Faigley, I. (1985) Nonacademic writing: The social perspective. In L. Odell & D. Goswami (Eds.), *Writing in nonacademic settings* (pp. 231-248). New York: Guilford.

Faigley, L. & Witte, S. (1981). Analyzing revision. *College Composition and Communication, 32*, 400-414.

Faigley, L., & Miller, T. (1982). What we learn from writing on the job. *College English, 44*, 557-569.

Farkas, D. (1995). Four research issues. *Technical Communication, 42*, 587-589.

Fish, S. (1995). *Professional correctness: Literary studies and political change*. Oxford: Oxford UP.

Fitschen, K. (1986). Effective advice to beginning writers: Revise the hard copy. *Teaching English in the two-year college, 13*, 104-108.

Flower, L., & Hayes, J. R. (1977). Problem-solving strategies and the writing process. *College English, 39*, 449-461.

Flower, L., & Hayes, J. R. (1980). The dynamics of composing: Making plans and juggling constraints. In L. W. Gregg & E. R. Steinberg (Eds.), *Cognitive processes in writing: An interdisciplinary approach* (pp. 31-50). Hillsdale, NJ: Erlbaum.

Flower, L., & Hayes, J. R. (1981a). A cognitive process theory of writing. *College Composition and Communication, 32*, 365-387.

Flower, L., & Hayes, J. R. (1981b). The pregnant pause: An inquiry into the nature of planning. *Research in the Teaching of English, 15*, 229-243.

Flower, L., & Hayes, J. R. (1984). Images, plans, and prose: The representation of meaning in writing. *Written Communication, 1*, 120-160.

Flower, L., Stein, V., Ackerman, J., Kantz, M. J., McCormick, K., & Peck, W. C. (1990). *Reading-to-write.: Exploring a cognitive and social process*. New York: Oxford.

Forman, J. (1991). Novices work on group reports: Problems in group writing and in computer-supported group writing. *Journal of Business and Technical Communication, 5*, 48-75.

Fortune, R. (1989). Visual and verbal thinking: Drawing and word processing software in writing instruction. In G. E. Hawisher & C. L. Selfe, (Eds.) *Critical perspectives on computers and composition instruction* (pp. 145-61). New York: Teachers College Press.

Fowler, H., Aaron, J., & Limburg, K. (1992). *The Little Brown handbook, Instructor's annotated edition*. New York: HarperCollins.

Galbraith, D. (1992). Conditions for discovery through writing. In M. Sharples (Ed.), *Computers and writing: Issues and implementations* (pp. 45-71). Dordrecht, Netherlands: Kluwer.

Gere, A. R. (1987). *Writing groups: History, theory, and implications*. Carbondale, IL: Southern Illinois University Press.

Goldstein, J. R., & Malone, E. L. (1985). Using journals to strengthen collaborative writing. *College English, 42*, 557-569.

Greenblatt, S. (1980). *Renaissance self-fashioning: From More to Shakespeare*. Chicago: University of Chicago Press.

Greenblatt, S. (1988a). *Representing the English renaissance*. Berkeley: University of California Press.

Greenblatt, S. (1988b). *Shakespearean negotiations: The circulation of social energy in renaissance England*. Berkeley, CA: University of California Press.

Greenblatt, S., & Gunn, G. (Eds.). (1992). *Redrawing the boundaries: The transformation of English and American literary studies*. New York: Modern Language Association.

Greene, J.C. (1957/58). Objectives and methods in intellectual history. *Mississippi Valley Historical Review, 44*, 58-74.

Haas, C. (1989a). Does the medium make a difference? A study of composing with pen and paper and with a computer. *Human-Computer Interaction, 4*, 149-169.

Haas, C. (1989b). How the writing medium shapes the writing process: Effects of word processing on planning. *Research in the Teaching of English, 23*, 181-207.

Haas, C. (1996). *Writing technology: Studies on the materiality of literacy*. Mahwah, NJ: Erlbaum.

Haas, C., & Hayes, J. R. (1986). *Pen and paper vs the machine: Writers composing in hard copy and computer conditions*. (CDC Technical Report 16). Pittsburgh, PA: Communication Design Center, Carnegie-Mellon University.

Hacker, D. (1994).*The Bedford handbook for writers*. Boston: Bedford, of St. Martin's Press.

Hacker, D., & Renshaw, B. (1979). *A practical guide for writers*. Boston: Little, Brown.

Hagge, J. (1995). Early engineering writing textbooks and the anthropological complexity of disciplinary discourse. *Written Communication, 12*, 439-491.

Halio, M. P. (1990). Student writing: Can the machine maim the message? *Academic Computing*, January, 16-19, 45.

Halliday, M. A. K. (1978). *Language as social semiotic: The social interpretation of language and meaning*. Baltimore: University Park Press.

Halliday, M. A. K. (1987). Spoken and written modes of meaning. In R. Horowitz & S. J. Samuels (Eds.), *Comprehending oral and written language* (pp. 55-82). New York: Academic Press.

Hammond, K., & Allen, J. Jr. (1953). *Writing clinical reports*. Englewood Cliffs, NJ: Prentice-Hall.

Harpold, T. (1991). Threnody: Psychoanalytic digressions on the subject of hypertexts. In P. Delany & G. Landow (Eds.), *Hypermedia and literary studies* (pp. 171-81).Cambridge, MA: MIT.

Harris, M. (1989). Composing behaviors of one- and multi-draft writers. *College English*, 51, 174-191.

Hartwell, P. (1979). Teaching arrangement: A pedagogy. *College English*, *40*, 548-554.

Harwell, G. (1960). *Technical communication*. New York: Macmillan.

Hawisher, G. E. (1987). Research update: Writing and word processing. *Computers and Composition*, 5, 7-23.

Hawisher, G. E. (1989). Research and recommendations for computers and composition. In G. E. Hawisher & C.L. Selfe, (Eds.) *Critical perspectives on computers and composition: Teaching and research in the virtual age* (pp.44-69) Portsmouth, NH: Boynton/Cook.

Hawisher, G. E. (1991). Connecting the visual and the verbal. In W. Wrensch (Ed.), *Lessons for the computer age* (pp. 129-132). Urbana, IL: NCTE.

Hawisher, G. E. (1994). Blinding insights: Classification schemes and software for literacy instruction. In C.L. Selfe & S. Hilligoss (Eds.) *Literacy and computers: The complications of teaching and learning with technology* (pp.37-55). New York: Modern Language Association.

Hayes, J., & Flower, L. (1980). Identifying the organization of writing processes. In L. W. Gregg & E. R. Steinberg (Eds.) *Cognitive processes in writing: An interdisciplinary approach* (pp. 3-30) Hillsdale: Erlbaum.

Hayes-Roth, N., & Hayes-Roth, F. (1979). A cognitive model of planning. *Cognitive Science*, *3*, 275-310.

Hays, R. (1965). *Principles of technical writing*. Reading, MA: Addison-Wesley.

Hedden, C. (1992). Hypertext and collaboration: Observations on Edward Barrett's philosophy. *Technical Communication Quarterly*, *I*, 27-41.

Heim, M. (1987). *Electric language: A philosophical study of word processing*. New Haven, CT: Yale.

Heim, M. (1993). *The metaphysics of virtual reality*. New York: Oxford.

Hill, D. J. (1990/1877). *The science of rhetoric*. New York. Excerpted in P. Bizzell & B. Herzberg (Eds.), *The rhetorical tradition* (pp. 877-881). Boston, MA: Bedford Books, of St. Martin's Press.

Hillocks, G. (1986). *Research on written composition: New directions for teaching*. Urbana, IL: National Conference on Research on English and ERIC-RCS.

Horton, S. R. (1982). *Thinking through writing*. Baltimore: Johns Hopkins.

Horton, W., Taylor, L., Ignacio, A., & Holt, N. I. (1996). *The Web page design cookbook*. New York: Wiley.

Houp, K., Pearsall, T., & Tebeaux, E, with Redish, J. (1995). *Reporting technical information*. Boston: Allyn & Bacon.

Hult, C., & Harris, J. (1987). *A writer's introduction to word processing*. Belmont, CA: Wadsworth.

Humphrey, D. (1987). Computers and collaboration: Writing as a social skill. *Assembly on Computers in English Newsletter*, July-September, 3.

Hutchins, E., Hollan, J., Norman, D. (1986). Direct manipulation interfaces. In D. Norman & S.W. Draper (Eds.), *User-centered design: New perspectives on human-computer interaction* (pp. 87-124). Hillsdale, NJ: Erlbaum.

Illych, I. (1973). *Tools for conviviality.* New York: Harper & Row. <http://www.la.psu.edu/philo/illich/tools.html> (1998, September 6).

InfoDesign. (1998). (Email list). InfoDesign@wins.uva.nl

Innis, H. (1951). *The bias of communication.* Toronto: University of Toronto Press.

Irish, P. M., & Trigg, R. H. (1989). Supporting collaboration in hypermedia: Issues and experiences. In E. Barrett (Ed.), *The society of text: Hypertext, hypermedia, and the social construction of knowledge* (pp. 93-106). Cambridge, MA: M.I.T. Press.

Jackson, S. L. (1974). *Libraries and librarianship in the West: A brief history.* New York: McGraw-Hill.

Johnson, J. (1992). *The Bedford guide to the research process.* New York: St. Martins Press.

Johnson, S. (1997). *Interface culture: How new technology transforms the way we create and communicate.* New York: HarperCollins.

Johnson-Eilola, J. (1994). Reading and writing in hypertext: Vertigo and euphoria. In C.L. Selfe & S. Hilligoss (Eds.) *Literacy and computers: The complications of teaching and learning with technology* (pp. 195-219). New York: Modern Language Association.

Jordan, J. (1965). *Using rhetoric.* New York, Harper & Row.

Joyce, M. (1988). Siren shapes: Exploratory and constructive hypertexts. *Academic Computing*, November, 10-15.

Kaplan, N. (1991). Ideology, technology, and the future of writing instruction. In G. E. Hawisher & C.L. Selfe (Eds.), *Evolving perspectives on computers and composition studies: Questions for the 1990s.* Urbana, IL: NCTE.

Kaplan, N., & Moulthrop, S. (1990) Computers and controversy: Other ways of seeing. *Computers and Composition, 7,* 89-102.

Kaplan, N., & Moulthrop, S. (1993). Seeing through the interface: Computers and the future of composition. In G. P. Landow & P. Delany (Eds.) *The digital word: Text-based computing in the humanities* (pp. 253-270). Cambridge, MA: MIT Press.

Kaufer, D. S., Fleming, D., Werner, M., & Sinsheimer-Weeks, A. (1993). Collaborative argument across the visual-verbal interface. *Technical Communication Quarterly, 2,* 37-49.

Kellogg, R. T. (1986). Writing method and productivity of science and engineering faculty. *Research in Higher Education, 25,* 147-163.

Kellogg, R. T. (1988). Attentional overload and writing performance: Effects of rough draft and outline strategies. *Journal of Experimental Psychology: Learning, Memory, and Cognition, 14,* 355-365.

Kellogg, R. T. (1994). *The psychology of writing.* New York: Oxford.

Kennedy, M. L. (1985). The composing process of college students writing from sources. *Written Communication, 2,* 434-456.

Kiesler, S., Siegel, J., & McGuire, T. (1988). Social psychological aspects of computer-mediated communication. In I. Greif (Ed.) *Computer-supported cooperative work* (pp. 657-682). San Mateo, CA: Morgan Kaufman.

Knoblauch, C. H., & Brannon, L. (1984). *Rhetorical traditions and the teaching of writing*. Upper Montclair, NJ: Boynton.

Kostelnick, C. (1989a) Process paradigms in design and composition: Affinities and directions. *College Composition and Communication, 40*, 267-281.

Kostelnick, C. (1989b). Visual rhetoric: A reader-oriented approach to graphics and designs. *The Technical Writing Teacher, 16*, 77-88.

Kostelnick, C. (1990). Typographical design, modernist aesthetics, and professional communication. *Journal of Business and Technical Communication, 4*, 5-24.

Kostelnick, C. (1994). From pen to print: The new visual landscape of professional communication. *Journal of Business and Technical Communication, 8*, 91-117.

Kostelnick, C. (1996). Supra-Textual design: The visual rhetoric of whole documents. *Technical Communication Quarterly, 5*, 9-34.

Kremers, M. (1990). Sharing authority on a synchronous network: The case for riding the beast. In M. Kremers & J. K. Peyton, (Eds.) *Papers from the fifth Computers and Writing Conference* (pp. 33-44). (Special issue of *Computers and Composition, 7*).

Krey, I., & Metzler, B., with Popham, E. (1968). *Effective writing for business*. New York: Harcourt, Brace.

Kuhlthau, C. C. (1988). Longitudinal case studies of the information search process of users in libraries. *Library & Information Science Research, 10*, 257-304.

Lakoff, G., & Johnson, M. (1980). Conceptual metaphor in everyday language. *Journal of Philosophy, 77*, 453-484.

Landauer, T. K. (1995). *The trouble with computers: Usefulness, usability, and productivity*. Cambridge, MA: MIT.

Landow, G. P. (1992). *Hypertext: The convergence of contemporary critical theory and technology*. Baltimore: Johns Hopkins.

Landow, G. P., & Delany, P. (Eds.). (1993). *The digital word: Text-based computing in the humanities*. Cambridge, MA: MIT Press.

Lanham, R. (1989) The electronic word: Literary study and the digital revolution. *New Literary History, 20*, 265-90.

Lanham, R. (1990). Foreword. In C. Handa (Ed.) *Computers and community: Teaching composition in the twenty-first century* (pp. xiii-xv). Portsmouth, NH: Boynton/Cook.

Lanham, R. (1993). *The electronic word: Democracy, technology, and the arts*. Chicago: University of Chicago Press.

Larson, R. (1996). Co-citation analysis and the WWW. <http://sherlock.berkeley.edu/asis96/node4.html> (1998, August 30).

Lay, M., Wahlstrom, B., Duin, A., Little, S., Selfe, C., Selzer, J., Rude, C., & Doheny-Farina, S. (1995). *Technical communication*. Chicago: Irwin.

Leggett, G., Mead, D., & Charvat, W. (1960). *Prentice Hall handbook for writers*. Englewood Cliffs, NJ: Prentice Hall.

Leggett, G., Mead, D., & Kramer, M. (1991). *Prentice Hall handbook for writers* (Eleventh Edition). Englewood Cliffs, NJ: Prentice Hall.

Lester, J. (1990). *Writing research papers, A complete guide*. Glenview, IL: Scott, Foresman.

Lodewijks, H. (1982). Self-regulated versus teacher-provided sequencing of information in learning from text. In A. Flammer & W. Kintsch (Eds.) *Discourse processing* (pp.509-20). Amsterdam: North-Holland.

Loehr, L. (1995). Composing in groups: The concept of authority in cross-functional project teamwork. *IEEE Transactions on Professional Communication, 38,* 83-94.

Lynch, K. (1960). *The image of the city.* Cambridge: MIT Press.

Mabrito, M. (1992). Real-time computer network collaboration: Case studies of business writing students. *Journal of Business and Technical Communication, 6,* 316-336.

Mager, R. F. (1988). *Making instruction work, or skillbloomers.* Belmont, CA: Lake.

Mahaney, W. (1981). *Workbook of current English.* Glenview, IL: Scott, Foresman.

Mandel, T. (1996). *The elements of user interface design.* New York: Wiley.

Mandler, J. M. (1984). *Stories, scripts, and scenes: Aspects of schema theory.* Hillsdale, NJ: Erlbaum.

Mansfield, C., & Bahniuk, M. (1981). *Writing business letters and reports.* Indianapolis, IN: Bobbs-Merrill Educational Publishing.

Marckwardt, A., & Cassidy, F. (1960). *Scribner handbook of English,* 3rd Edition. New York: Charles Scribner's Sons.

Markel, M. (1984). *Technical writing: Situations and strategies.* New York: St. Martin's Press.

Martin, H. (1957). *The logic and rhetoric of exposition.* New York: Rinehart.

Matson, E. (1996). The seven sins of deadly meetings. *Fast Company, 1,* 123. <http://www.fastcompany.com/online/02/meetings.html> (1998, August 24).

Mazumdar, S., Bao, W, Yuan, Z., & Price, J. (1998). Adding Semantics to SGML Databases. Presentation at Electronic Publishing '98 Conference, Saint Mâlo, France (April 1-4, 1998), included in *Electronic publishing, Proceedings of the Electronic Publishing '98 Conference (Lecture notes in computer science* series). Berlin: Springer-Verlag. (In press).

McCarthy, J. (1981). History of LISP. In R. L. Wexelblat (Ed.), *History of programming languages* (pp. 173-185). New York: Academic Press.

McCarthy, L. P. (1985). A stranger in strange lands: A college student writing across the curriculum. Unpublished dissertation, University of Pennsylvania. (University Microfilms No. 8515414). <http://www.lib.umi.com/dxweb/details?doc_no=788851> (1998, August 29).

McCutchen, D. (1986). Domain knowledge and linguistic knowledge in the development of writing ability. *Journal of Memory and Language, 25,* 431-444.

McDonald, P.B. (1929). *English and science.* New York: Van Nostrand.

McKee, B. (1972). Do professional writers use an outline when they write? *Technical Communication, 19,* 10-13.

McKee, B. K. (1974/75). Types of outlines used by technical writers. *Journal of English Teaching Techniques, 7,* 30-36.

McLuhan, M. (1962). *The Gutenberg galaxy.* Toronto: University of Toronto.

McLuhan, M. (1964a). *Understanding media: The extensions of man.* New York: Signet. Reprinted 1996. Cambridge, MA: MIT.

McLuhan, M. (1964b). Introduction to reprint of Innis, H., *The bias of communication*. Toronto: University of Toronto Press.

Messer-Davidow, E., Shumway, D., & D. J. Sylvan. (Eds.). (1993). *Knowledges: Historical and critical studies in disciplinarity*. Charlottesville, VA: University of Virginia Press.

Meyrowitz, N., & van Dam, A. (1982). Interactive editing systems: Parts I and II. *ACM Computing Surveys, 14*, 321-415.

Microsoft. (1997). *Microsoft encarta 97 encyclopedia*. Redmond, WA: Microsoft.

Miller, G. A. (1956). The magical number seven, plus or minus two: Some limits on our capacity for processing information. *Psychological Review, 63*, 81-97.

Miller, P. (1939). *The New England mind: The seventeenth century*. (Re-issued 1954). Cambridge, MA: Harvard.

Mills, G., & Walter, J. (1962). *Technical writing*. New York: Holt, Rinehart, & Winston.

Mills, G., & Walter, J. (1978). *Technical writing* (Fourth Edition). New York: Holt, Rinehart, & Winston.

Mischel, T. (1974). *A case study of a twelfth grade writer*. Research in the Teaching of English, 8, 303-314.

Moberg, G. (1986). *Writing on computers in English composition*. New York: Writing Consultant.

Mok, C. (1996). *Designing business: Multiple media, multiple disciplines*. San Jose, CA: Adobe.

Montaigne, M. de. (1580). Sur Cicero. *Essais*. Paris.

Moran, C. (1990). The computer-writing room: Authority and control. *Computers and Composition, 7*, 61-69.

Moulthrop, S. (1989). In the zones: Hypertext and the politics of interpretation. *Writing on the Edge 1*, 18-27.

Murray, D. M. (1985). The essential delay: When a writer's block isn't. In M. Rose (Ed.) *When a writer can't write* (pp. 219-226). New York: Guilford Press.

Myers, L. M. (1955). *Guide to American English*. (Prentice-Hall English Composition and Introduction to Literature Series). Englewood Cliffs, NJ: Prentice-Hall.

Naylor, J. (1942). *Informative writing*. New York: Macmillan.

Nelson, J. (1940). *Writing the technical report*. New York: McGraw.

Nelson, J. (1992). *Constructing a research paper: A study of students' goals and approaches*. (Tech Report No. 59). Berkeley, CA: University of California, Center for the Study of Writing.

Nelson, T. H. (1967). Getting it out of our system. In G. Schechter (Ed.), *Information retrieval: A critical review* (pp. 191-210). Washington, DC: Thompson.

Newell, A., & Simon, H. A. (1972). *Human problem-solving*. Englewood Cliffs, NJ: Prentice Hall.

Nickerson, R. S., Perkins, D. N., & Smith, E. E. (1985). *The teaching of thinking*. Hillsdale, NJ: Erlbaum.

Nielsen, J. (In press, 1999). *Designing websites with authority: Secrets of an information architect*. Indianapolis, IN: New Riders.

North, S. M. (1987). *The making of knowledge in composition: Portrait of an emerging field*. Upper Montclair, N.J: Boynton/Cook.

NUA Internet Surveys. (1998). (Electronic newsletter and Web site).. Ireland: Nua, Ltd. <http://www.nua.net/surveys/how_many_online/world.html> (1998, August 25).

Nystrand, M., Greene, S., & Wiemelt, J. (1993). Where did composition studies come from? An intellectual history. *Written Communication, 10,* 267-333.

Oliu, W., Brusaw, C., & Alred, G. (1995). *Writing that works: How to write effectively on the job.* New York: St. Martin's Press.

Olsen, L.A. (1989). Computer-based writing and communication: Some implications for technical communication activities. *Journal of Technical Writing and Communication, 19,* 97-118.

Olson, D. R. (1976). Culture, technology, and intellect. In L. B. Resnick (Ed.), *The nature of intelligence* (pp. 189-202). Hillsdale, NJ: Erlbaum.

Olson, G. M., & Atkins, D. E. (1990). Supporting collaboration with adanced multimedia electronic mail: The NSF EXPRES project. In J. Galegher, R. E. Kraut, & C. Egido (Eds.), *Intellectual teamwork: Social and technological foundations of cooperative work,* pp. 429-451. Hillsdale, NJ: Erlbaum.

Ong, W. J., S. J. (1958). *Ramus, method, and the decay of dialogue: From the art of discourse to the art of reason.* Cambridge, MA: Harvard.

Ong, W. J., S. J. (1982). *Orality and literacy: The technologizing of the word.* New York: Methuen.

Papert, S. (1980). *Mindstorms: Children, computers, and powerful ideas.* New York: Basic.

Papert, S. (1997). *The connected family: Bridging the digital generation gap.* Boston: Longstreet.

Pearsall, T., & Cunningham, D. (1978). *How to write for the world of work.* New York: Holt, Rinehart, & Winston.

Perl, S. (1979). The composing processes of unskilled college writers. *Research in the Teaching of English, 13* (4) 317-336.

Perrin, P. (1955). *Writer's guide and index to English.* Chicago: Scott, Foresman.

Pianko, S. H. (1979). A description of the composing processes of college freshman writers. *Research in the Teaching of English, 13,* 5-22.

Pickett, N., & Laster, A. (1984). *Technical English: Writing, reading, and speaking.* New York: Harper & Row.

Pliny the Elder. (1944/1977). *Natural history, I, Books 1-2* (H. Rackham, Trans.). (Loeb Classical Library #330). . Cambridge, MA: Harvard.

Pliny the Elder. (1998) *Historia naturalis* (K. Mayhoff, Ed. , 1897-1908; B. Thayer, Ed., 1998) <http://www.ukans.edu/history/index/europe/ancient_rome/E/Roman/Texts/Pliny_the_El der/home*.html> (1998, August 31).

Plumb, C. (1990). What can technical writers learn from good conversation? *Journal of Technical Writing and Communication, 20,* 201-209.

Plung, D. L. (1982). The advantages of sentence outlining. *Technical Communication, 29,* 8-11.

Podis, J. M., & Podis, L.A. (1990). Identifying and teaching rhetorical plans for arrangement. *College Composition and Communication, 41,* 430-442.

Podis, L. A. (1980). Teaching arrangement: Defining a more practical approach. *College Composition and Communication, 31,* 197-204.

Porter, J. E. (1986). Intertextuality and the discourse community. *Rhetoric Review*, 5, 34-47.

Price, J. (1977). *Video visions: A medium discovers itself.* New York: New American Library.

Price, J. (1992). How do writers really collaborate? *IPCC 92 conference record* (pp. 460-463). Santa Fe, NM: IEEE.

Price, J. (1997a). Structuring complex interactive documents. Introduction to a special issue (same title) of the *IEEE Transactions on Professional Communication*, July, 69-77.

Price, J. (1997b). Using complexity theory to understand what's happening to technical communication. *IPCC 97 proceedings, October 22-25, 1997, Salt Lake City, Utah, 17-27* (pp. 17-28). Salt Lake City, UT: IEEE Professional Communication Society..

Price, J. (1997c). How electronic outlining can help you create online materials. *Conference proceedings, 15th annual international conference on computer documentation, October 19-22, 1997, Salt Lake City, Utah* (pp. 211-221). Salt Lake City, UT: Association for Computing Machinery (ACM), Special Interest Group on Systems Documentation (SIGDOC).

Price, J. (1997d). Electronic outlining as a tool for making writing visible. *Computers and Composition*, December, 409-427.

Price, J. (1998). Complexity theory as a way of understanding our role in the World-Wide Web. *STC 45th annual conference proceedings* (pp. 207-209). Anaheim, CA: STC.

Price, J., & Korman, H. (1993). *How to communicate technical information.* Menlo Park, CA: Benjamin/Cummings.

Price, J. & Urban, L. (1984). *The definitive word-processing book.* New York: Penguin.

Ramus, P. (1543). *Dialectiones partitiones.* Paris. Portions of English translation in P. Miller (1939), *The New England mind: The seventeenth century*, Cambridge, MA: Harvard, quoted in Batschelet, M. W., (1988), Plain style and scientific style: The influence of the Puritan plain style sermon on early American science writers. *Journal of Technical Writing and Communication, 18*, 287-295.

Rodrigues, D., & Rodrigues, R. (1986). *Teaching writing with a word processor.* Urbana, IL: National Council of Teachers of English.

Rogers, R. L. (1986). Preparing course materials with an outline processor. *Teaching of Psychology, 13*, 154-155.

Rose, M. (1980). Rigid rules, inflexible plans, and the stifling of language: A cognitivist analysis of writer's block. *College Composition and Communication, 31*, 389-401.

Rosenfeld, L., & Morville, P. (1998). *Information architecture for the World Wide Web.* Sebastapol, CA: O'Reilly.

Rouse, R. H., & Rouse, M. A. (1989). Wax tablets. *Language and Communication, 9*, 175-191.

Rubens, P. (Ed.). (1992). *Science and technical writing: A manual of style.* New York: Henry Holt.

Rubin, D. L. (1988). Introduction: Four dimensions of social construction in written communication. In B. A. Raforth & D. L. Rubin (Eds.). *The social construction of written communication* (pp. 1-33). Norwood, NJ: Ablex.

Rude, C. D. (1988). Format in instructional manuals: Applications of existing research. *Journal of Business and Technical Communication, 2,* 63-77.

Ruskiewicz, J. (1988) Word and image: The next revolution. *Computers and Composition, 5,* 9-16.

Rymer, J. (1993). Collaboration and conversation in learning communities: The discipline and the classroom. In. N. R. Blyler & C. Thralls (Eds.) *Professional communication: The social perspective* (pp. 179-195). Newbury Park, CA: Sage.

Samuels, M. (1989). *The technical writing process.* New York: Oxford.

Sandman, P., Klompus, C, & Yarrison, B. (1985). *Scientific and technical writing.* New York: Holt, Rinehart, & Winston.

Santmyers, S. (1949). *Practical report writing.* Scranton, PA: International Textbook Company.

Scardamalia, M., & Bereiter, C. (1983). The development of evaluation, diagnostic, and remedial capabilities in children's composing. In M. Matlew (Ed.), *The psychology of written language: A developmental approach* (pp. 67-95). London: Wiley.

Schank, R. & Abelson, R. (1977). *Scripts, plans, goals, and understanding.* Hillsdale: Erlbaum.

Schmidt, S. (1983). *Creating the technical report.* Englewood Cliffs, NJ: Prentice-Hall.

Schneider, M.L. (1990). Collaborative learning: A concept in search of a definition. *Issues in Writing, 3,* 26-39.

Schoeck, R. J. (1983). Lawyers and rhetoric in sixteenth-century England. In J. J. Murphy (Ed.), *Renaissance eloquence.* Berkeley, CA: University of California Press.

Schriver, K. A. (1997). *Dynamics of document design.* New York: Wiley.

Schubert, L. (1948). *A guide for oral communication.* New York: Prentice-Hall.

Schwartz, H. (1985). *Interactive writing: Composing with a word processor.* New York: Holt.

Selber, S. A. (1995). Metaphorical perspectives on hypertext. *IEEE Transactions on Professional Communication, 38,* 59-67.

Shelton, J. (1995). *Handbook for technical writing.* Lincolnwood, IL: NTC Business Books.

Sherman, A. (1970). *The research paper guide.* West Haven, CT: Pendulum Press.

Sherman, T. (1955). *Modern technical writing.* New York: Prentice Hall.

Sherman, T. (1966). *Modern technical writing* (Second Edition). Englewood Cliffs, NJ: Prentice-Hall.

Shneiderman, B. (1983). Direct manipulation: A step beyond programming languages. *IEEE Computer, 16,* 57-69.

Shneiderman, B. (1992). *Designing the user interface: Strategies for effective human-computer interaction.* Reading, MA: Addison-Wesley.

Sinfield, A. (1992). *Faultlines.* Berkeley, Los Angeles: Oxford UP.

Slatin, J. M. (1990). Reading hypertext: Order and coherence in a new medium. *College English, 52,* 870-83.

Smart, W., & Lang, D. (1943). *Smart's handbook of effective writing.* New York. Harper & Brothers.

Smith, K. L. (1990). Collaborative and interactive writing for increasing communication skills. *Hispania, 73*, pp. 77-87.

Smith, C. F. (1994). Hypertextual thinking. In C. L. Selfe & S. Hilligoss (Eds.), *Literacy and computers: The complications of teaching and learning with technology* (pp. 264-281). New York: Modern Language Association.

Smith, R. (1940). *Learning to write in college*. Boston: Little, Brown.

Society for Technical Communication, Information Design Special Interest Group. (1998). *Design Matters*. (Newsletter). <http://stc.org/pics/idsig/> (1998, August 26).

Sommers, N. (1980) Revision strategies of student writers and experienced adult writers. *College Composition and Communication, 31*, 378-388.

Sommers, N., & McQuade, D. (1984). *Student writers at work: The Bedford prizes*. New York: St. Martin's.

Stallard, C. (1974). An analysis of the behavior of good student writers. *Research in the Teaching of English, 8*, 206-218.

Stein, V. (1990). Exploring the cognition of reading-to-write. In L. Flower, V. Stein, J. Ackerman, M. J. Kantz, K. McCormick, & W.C. Peck (Eds.), *Reading-to-write: Exploring a cognitive and social process* (pp. 119-143). New York: Oxford.

Stotsky, S. (1990). On planning and writing plans—Or beware of borrowed theories! *College Composition and Communication, 41*, 37-57.

Stratman, J. F. (1990). The emergence of legal composition as a field of inquiry: Evaluating the prospects. *Review of Educational Research, 2*, 153-235.

Streitz, N., Rizk, A., & Andre, J. (Eds.). (1990). *Hypertext: Concepts, systems, applications. Proceedings of the European conference on hypertext, INRIA, Versailles, France, November, 1990*. Cambridge, UK: Cambridge University Press.

Sypherd, W., Fountain, A., & Gibbens, V. (1957). *Manual of technical writing: A revision and extension of The engineer's manual of English*. Chicago: Scott, Foresman.

Taylor, B. M., & Beach, R. W. (1984). The effects of text structure instruction on middle-grade students' comprehension and production of expository text. *Reading Research Quarterly, 19*, 134-136.

Thomas, B. (1991). *The new historicism and other old-fashioned topics*. Princeton, NJ: Princeton University Press.

Thomas, J. D. (1949). *Composition for technical students*. New York: Scribner's.

Tomlinson, B. (1988). Tuning, tying, and training texts: Metaphors for revision. *Written Communication, 5*, 58-81.

Trzyna, T., & Batschelet, M. (1987). *Writing for the technical professions*. Belmont, CA: Wadsworth.

Tuman, M. C. (1992). *Word perfect: Literacy in the computer age*. Pittsburgh: University of Pittsburgh.

Tuttle, R., & Brown, C. (1956). *Writing useful reports: Principles and applications*. New York: Appleton-Century-Crofts.

Ulmer, G. (1989). *Teletheory: Grammatology in the age of video*. New York: Routledge.

U.S. Department of Education, Office of Special Education Programs, Office of Special Education and Rehabilitative Services, with the National School

Boards Association. (1997). *Technology for students with disabilities: A decision maker's resource guide.* U.S. Department of Education: Washington, D.C. <http://www.empowermentzone.com/techstud.txt> (1998, August 24).

USGS. (1957) *Suggestions to authors of the reports of the United States Geological Survey,* Fifth Edition. Washington, DC: United States Geological Survey.

van Dijk, T. A., & Kintsch, W. (1983). *Strategies of discourse comprehension.* New York: Academic.

Volosinov, V. N. (1973/1929). *Marxism and the philosophy of language* (L. Matejka & I. R. Titunik, trans.). Cambridge, MA: Harvard University Press.

Vygotsky, L. (1962/1934). *Thought and language.* (E. Hanfmann, Ed., G. Vakar, Trans.). Cambridge, MA: MIT.

Waern, Y. (1989). *Cognitive aspects of computer-supported tasks.* New York: Wiley.

Wagner, B. J. (1994). An easy outlining approach for producing solidly structured, audience-directed reports. *Journal of Business and Technical Communication, 8,* 475-482.

Walvoord, B. E., Anderson, V.J., Breihan, J. R., McCarthy, L. P., Robison, S. M., & Sherman, A. K. (1995). Functions of outlining among college students in four disciplines. *Research in the Teaching of English, 29,* 390-421.

Ward, D. A. (1991). The "reader's outline": A tool for global revision. *Journal of Teaching Writing, 10,* 201-215.

Ward, R. (1968). *Practical technical writing.* New York: Alfred Knopf.

Warriner, J. (1950). *English grammar and composition: Complete course.* New York: Harcourt Brace Jovanovich.

Warriner, J., Mersand, J., & Griffith, F. (1958). *English grammar and composition.* New York: Harcourt Brace Jovanovich.

Weaver, R., with Beal, R. (1967). *Rhetoric and composition.* New York: Holt, Rinehart, & Winston.

Weidenborner, S., & Caruso, D. (1990). *Writing research papers, A guide to the process.* New York: St. Martin's Press.

Weisman, H. (1962). *Basic technical writing.* Columbus, OH: Charles E. Merrill Books.

Weiss, E. (1982). *The writing system for engineers and scientists.* Englewood Cliffs, NJ: Prentice-Hall.

Wellborn, G., Green, L., & Nall, K. (1961). *Technical writing.* Boston: Houghton Mifflin.

Whately, R. (1990/1928). *Elements of rhetoric.* Excerpted in P. Bizzell & B. Herzberg, *The rhetorical tradition* (pp. 831-858). Boston, MA: Bedford Books, of St. Martin's Press.

Wicker, C., & Albrecht, W. (1960). *The American technical writer: A handbook of objective writing.* New York: American Book.

Wilcox, R. (1977). *Communication at work: Writing and speaking.* Boston: Houghton Mifflin.

Willinsky, J. (1994). *Empire of words: The reign of the OED.* Princeton, NJ: Princeton UP.

Wilson, T. (1990/1553). *The arte of rhetorique.* Excerpts reprinted in P. Bizzell & B. Herzberg (Eds.), *The rhetorical tradition* (pp. 584-621). Boston, MA: Bedford Books, of St. Martin's Press.

Winer, D. (1988). Outliners and programming. <http://www.scripting.com/dwiner/outlinersProgramming.html> (1998, August 20).

Winograd, T., & Flores, F. (1986). *Understanding computers and cognition: A new foundation for design*. Reading, MA: Addison-Wesley.

Witte, S. P. (1983). Topical structure and revision: An exploratory study. *College Composition and Communication, 34*, 313-341.

Witte, S. P. (1987). Pre-text and composing. *College Composition and Communication, 38*, 397-425.

Witte, S. P. (1992). Context, text and intertext: Toward a constructivist semiotic of writing. *Written Communication, 9*, 237-308.

Wurman, R. S. (1996). *Information architects*. Zurich: Graphis Press.

Young, M. (1989). *The technical writer's handbook: Writing with style and clarity*. Mill Valley, CA: University Science Books.

Young, R. L. (1991). A dialogue user interface architecture. In J. W. Sullivan & S. W. Tyler, (Eds.), *Intelligent user interfaces* (pp. 157-176). Reading, MA: ACM Press, Addison-Wesley.

Young, R., Becker, A., & Pike, K. (1970). *Rhetoric: discovery and change*. New York: Harcourt Brace.

Zuboff, S. (1988). *In the age of the smart machine: The future of work and power*. New York: Basic.

Author Index

Subject Index